We Are Family

AN ASSEMBLY BOOK FOR 4–8 YEAR-OLDS

Geoff Davies

DEDICATION

For Emily Joy
1980-1983

Acknowledgements

To my wife, Mollie, for reading the stories and for her thoughts on cover design; Ann Allen, Head of Music at Parsons Down Junior School, Thatcham for writing the music to the new version of 'A School Creed' on page 227; Mrs Janice Schofield, Headteacher, Parsons Down Infant School, Thatcham, for her advice and in assisting with resources; my son Philip, and Mrs Jenny Rankin, for their assistance in obtaining information.

Copyright acknowledgements

The author and publishers are grateful for permission to reproduce copyright material: Mrs Sarah Matthews for 'St David's Day' by Stanley Cook, © the estate of Stanley Cook; John Cotton for 'Christmas Eve Night'; Martin Wiley and Ian McMillan for 'My Dad Said'; all published in *Let's Celebrate* (ed. John Foster) by Oxford University Press; and Coral Rumble for 'Little Lies', published in *Poems About Me* by Wayland Publishers. Every effort has been made to contact any copyright holder who has not been acknowledged.

CONTENTS

Subjects marked * may need a sensitive approach. Teachers should always be aware of the composition of their audience before conducting an assembly.

PART II

SPECIAL DAYS: FESTIVALS AND CELEBRATIONS TRADITIONAL TO THE BRITISH ISLES

PART III

SPECIAL DAYS: FESTIVALS AND CELEBRATIONS ORIGINATING IN CULTURES NOT NATIVE TO THE BRITISH ISLES

PART IV

APPENDICES

About this book

All children at all schools are still bound, by law, to participate in 'a daily act of corporate worship'.which varies in content and character according to the child population to whom it is addressed.

Teachers recognise that the practicalities of school life lead to the school assembly often being a 'corporate act' without being patently religious in content or character.Neither do schools always hold assemblies at the start of the school day. Denominational schools, of whatever religious persuasion, do, as we know, have an obligation to ensure that their gatherings are religious in character.

What is important is that the assembly content and conduct shall be appropriate for the children who participate – all teachers know that what is meaningful for children new to the world of school is totally unsuitable for Year 6 children with one eye on the next stage of their education.

We Are Family then, is designed to cater for the children up to the end of Key Stage 1, who used to be lovingly known as 'Infants', although part of the book may be useful in the first year of Key Stage 2.

The aim of *We Are Family* is to offer resource material upon which teachers can draw to suit their own requirements.

The whole assembly structure may be used, part of it, or the stories alone, as a core for the teacher's own activity during assembly time or at any other time of day. Exactly how the book is used is up to whoever decides to use it.

Each assembly takes as its theme the day-to-day concerns and the social development of young children as members of the family of school, the family at home and the wider family of society. None of the assemblies is directly related to any actual religious dogma of any faith; desirable human qualities, such as honesty and gentle behaviour are not peculiar to any particular creed.

Some topics may require sensitive handling and are marked with a *. Individual schools will know best.

Those assemblies that do appear to be related to a particular faith ('Celebrations at the time of') are included as a recognition of the different traditions and cultures now manifest in the United Kingdom as part of our whole contemporary culture. That is to say, the 'Celebration Assemblies' centre on one aspect of the positive values of the teachings of a particular faith.

The 'assembly pattern' begins with *Let's talk*, suggested dialogue between adult and children.

This session is suggested so that children may, under guidance, discuss their own limited skills, experience and knowledge and put forward opinions (rudimentary though we adults may think they are) regarding the theme under consideration.

'Leading' questions to prompt children's responses are suggested rather than prescribed. Many teachers, no doubt, will make up their own minds about the composition of this element of the assembly, preferring to make their own opening gambits – it may that they have a specific instance with which to deal or they may be following up some school activity or incident.

Inevitably, the degree of child participation in any assembly is related to the ethos of any particular school and cannot be formulated from outside the school situation. Any discussion is succeeded by mostly passive listening to stories (non-fiction narrative is used once only in this book). All are related to the theme of the assembly and many of them are allegories.

Every story carries a message, which may or may not be a 'moral', followed through, apart from in the early assemblies, by asking children to think about what they have heard and to give further opinions.

The first section, entitled *Share your thoughts with everyone,* will need initial encouragement and, probably later, limitation. After public discussion, if any, there follows a short period of personal reflection, as suggested in the Agreed Syllabus of most authorities – *Think quietly about* ... .

In Parts II and III (Celebrations), *Share your thoughts* and *Think quietly* are replaced by *A pause for thought.* No prayers are suggested for Part III, which is concerned with 'Special days traditional to Family whose cultures are not native to the British Isles'. The term 'British Isles' is preferred to 'United Kingdom' because the celebration of St Patrick's Day may relate to people who are citizens of the Irish Republic.

Songs to sing are mainly secular songs but some, especially those from the song book *Come & Praise*, may have sacred elements. Monotheistic prayers, using only the modes of address, 'Father', 'Father God', 'Lord' or 'Lord God', have been detached and placed in a separate Appendix 1.

For pre-school, Reception, Year 1 and Year 2 children, the keynote of any assembly should be sensible brevity. It should not be so brief as to be meaningless, but neither should it last long enough for little bodies to begin wriggling. Some teachers may consider that talking, listening, more talking, singingand, perhaps, praying *is* too much. In that case, it is best for the teacher-in-charge to select what is appropriate for their audience.

Even so, each assembly should attempt to deliver a message that will mean something to the children to whom it is addressed, and they should enjoy the experience of 'togetherness' as a school family.

Mood music – 'coming-in' and 'going-out' music – is suggested in Appendix 5 for those who have access to, or prefer to use, recorded music before, during or after the assembly.

If teachers do not have the time or the facilities to select particular pieces of music, then they might play something cheerful but calm, whether contemporary, classical or traditional – Musak is better than nothing at all.

The main limitation on the use of recorded music is the extent of the school's resource bank, the teacher's versatility, the demands on very limited non-contact time for preparation and powers of acquisition and persuasion.

Ultimately, you, headteacher, teacher or group leader, have to decide the character, content and frequency of your assemblies, and this book is intended to be more of a resource book rather than a word-by-word script.

But, however you use this or any other assembly book, you should resolve to make the assemblies that you conduct purposeful and enjoyable and not just a chore – so, go on, enjoy them yourself.

PART I
WE ARE FAMILY

THE FAMILY OF SCHOOL

1 Getting to know you

Theme

Welcome to new children.

Schools' policies for the first assembly at which new admissions are present vary widely. The first meeting of a new school year or term may be with a single class, a team, a department or the whole school. Whatever pattern you favour, this assembly should aim to make the point that a school is rather like one big family – preferably a happy one.

Let's talk

Who knows the name of this school?

It is our school – yours and mine.

It is like a big family with a lot of children and grown-ups.

Let me tell you about our school family.

(*Tell the children what you think they need to know about the school – anything that you think is relevant.*)

Time to listen

This is a story about a very big family. It is called:

Big Family, Strange House

Mrs Oldwoman and her forty children lived in a tiny cottage that was far too small for them all.

One morning, Mrs Oldwoman was surprised to see an enormous boot standing in the middle of her garden. Why it was in her garden, she could not imagine, nor can I.

As it seemed to belong to nobody, Mrs Oldwoman asked Mr Botch, the builder, to turn it into a house by building a roof, walls, stairs and chimney. Then the delighted family moved in.

The children all worked together to clean the boot-house and they all helped with the chores like bed-making and washing-up. They never, ever quarrelled – well, hardly ever – and they were all very happy. On cold nights they ate delicious soup that Mrs Oldwoman had cooked, then all the children went sleepily to bed.

Then, one moonlit night, everyone was woken by a loud noise, *Thumpety, plonkety, thumpety, plonkety!* Outside was a huge giant, tall enough to bump his head against the moon. He was making the strange noise because he was only wearing one boot.

The family were living in the giant's other boot! As you might expect, he picked up the boot and began to shake everything out on to the ground.

Just in time, Mr Stitch the shoemaker rushed out, saying he would make the giant a new pair of boots free of charge. The giant agreed, because he was not grumpy, really, and off he stumped, *Thumpety, plonkety, thumpety, plonkety.* When he returned a week later, he was thrilled with the new boots. Straight away, he took off his one old boot and left it on the village green.

Off he marched, *Thumpety, thumpety, thumpety, thumpety*, and nobody ever saw him again. The boot he left behind became the new village hall and everyone was pleased. Especially Mrs Oldwoman and her happy family.

The message is

A family is much happier when everyone does their share

Think quietly about

*Our own families at home

Songs to sing

The family of man	*Come & Praise* 69
Use your eyes	*Every Colour* 112
What's it like in the place where you live?	*Play School Song Book* 14
I belong to a family	*Sing it in the Morning* 3
Welcome home	*Tinderbox* 60

Prayers

Page 216

2 I won't eat you, you know!

Theme

Having confidence in grown-ups in school.

Some children new to the world of formal school may see the person who seems to be in charge as a daunting figure, perhaps more so if the person is a man. This is more likely in the larger school in which Reception, Year 1 and Year 2 make up a department (Key Stage 1) and the head teacher seems more remote. The new recruits usually come to realise in a short space of time that such adult figures of authority have only their welfare at heart and that their function is not to terrorise little children. This assembly is designed to accelerate such a realisation.

Of course, this assembly may not be at all necessary and those children who may have reservations about people in authority can be reassured in a one-to-one or small-group situation. In that case, just read them the story ...

Let's talk

Who is your teacher?

Who is the head teacher?

What does it mean when we say that the head teacher is in charge of this school?

Time to listen

This is a story about someone who is in charge of a lot of pixies called Brockles. It is called:

Bobkin Meets the Big Boss

Brockles are *very* small people, not much bigger than your big toe. I suppose you could say they were a kind of pixie and only children can see them. I have never actually seen one and I only know about them because a young friend of mine very kindly told me what they look like.

One pixie-day, Bobkin Brockle was in trouble.

His mother grumbled at him, 'Bobkin, *why* did you let Farmer Bungle's sheep into Granny Butterpin's garden yesterday? They ate every single cabbage. If you're not careful, someone will take you to the Big Boss Brockle at Biddley Bump and you won't like that.'

'I'm not scared of *him*,' sniggered Bobkin. 'See if I care.'

With that, he stuck out his tongue at his mother and ran out of the toadstool house. He went to Mr Billy Bugle's garden where he poked big holes in every one of the prize pumpkins that were growing in the garden. But who should come out of his house but ... Billy Bugle himself. He grabbed hold of Bobkin's long, pointed Brockle ear and dragged him to Biddley Bump, where stood an old conker tree with a little black door in its trunk.

The door opened and Billy Bugle pushed Bobkin through. Inside it was pitch dark and Bobkin stood, shivering with fright. Then the door slammed shut and a scary blue light in the roof came on. And there, standing in front of Bobkin was ... Big Boss Brockle, the tallest Brockle Bobkin had ever seen – almost as tall as a squirrel and wearing a bright yellow coat and a tall black hat.

He boomed, 'So, young Bobkin, you have been behaving very badly. Maybe I should ask my friend, Wizard Brocklebump, to turn you into an earwig? Or are you going to go on being naughty?' Bobkin shook his head so hard that it could easily have fallen off.

He squeaked 'Oh, no, Sir, your Greatness, Sir, I won't, please don't turn me into an earwig, I shall never be naughty again. I promise.'

Big Boss Brockle beamed a big smile and said, kindly, 'I am glad to hear it. Just go away and behave yourself. But the next time ...'

He disappeared and Bobkin found he was back in his own garden, not sure how he got there. But he did know that, although Big Boss Brockle was a scary sort of Very Important Person, he was also a very kind person.

Do you think Bobkin behaved himself after that?

The message is

People with important jobs are usually kind people and, although you should take notice of what they say, they would not want you to be afraid of them.

Think quietly about

What scares you about a grown-up – any grown-up?

Is there anything you can do about it – like telling someone you are *not* scared of them?

Songs to sing

The first time
I whistle a happy tune
We will take care of you
Can you hear?
Ten little squirrels
Mysteries

Sing a Silver Lining 13
Apusskidu 3
Every Colour 36
Harlequin 33
Okki-Tokki-Unga 40
Tinderbox 40

Prayers

Page 216

3 Working for our school family

Theme

The adults who work in a school.

Children starting school – and often those who have been for a while – do not always appreciate that there is more to a school than the teaching staff and their auxiliaries. The school would be a sorry place without the staff who do all the other things necessary to run it.

Let's talk

Tell me what you know about the grown-ups, besides the teachers, who work in this school.

Do they all work here when children are here?

Tell me about some of the jobs they do.

Time to listen

Nowadays, Red Indians are known as native Americans because they lived in America before anybody else.There was no such 'Red Indian' tribe as the Soso tribe in this story!

The Know-all Chief

Mighty Wind, Chief of the Soso tribe said to his wife, 'I think I make a good job of being chief. In fact, I could probably do everyone else's jobs just as well as they can.' Then Silent Cat put his head through the door and asked, 'Where is Oldbones, the medicine-man? My wife is ill and I need help.'

Mighty Wind said, 'He is away but don't worry, I shall make your wife better.'

After thinking for a minute, he said, 'Take your wife to bathe in the Crystal Pool.' It was just as well that Oldbones returned and told Silent Cat that his wife would have died in the freezing water and gave her some proper medicine which made her better. Then he told Mighty Wind to mind his own business and not to meddle in things he knew nothing about.

Then Sharp Knife said, 'Bright Spear, the Head Warrior is ill and we cannot practise shooting with bows and arrows. What can we do?'

'Oh, I can teach shooting,' cried the Chief. But his teaching was so bad that Sitting Cat shot Red Knife in the place where he sits down, and he told the Chief to mind his own business and not to meddle in things he knew nothing about. Mighty Wind 'helped' with canoe practice, hunting wolves and fishing for salmon, and each time somebody got hurt, and each time Mighty Wind was told not to meddle in things he knew nothing about.

At the end of the day, Chief Mighty Wind moaned to his squaw that it had been a rotten day and he was useless.

But she told him to stick to being Chief, as all he had to do was to look important and to make sure that everyone in the the tribe was a good neighbour. And he was good at that, she said.

She said, too, that it showed how that everyone in the tribe was important. Even the Chief.

The message is ...

Although everyone has a part to play, it is best if some jobs are left to people who know what they are doing.

Share your thoughts with everyone

How can children be useful in school?

Think quietly about

The hard work done by all the people who work in this school when there are no children here.

Songs to sing

Work calypso	*The Music Box Song Book* 21
Working together	*Every Colour* 37
Each day different	*Harlequin* 43
Can anyone tell me that?	*Tinderbox* 6
Sing a song of people	*Tinderbox* 18

Prayers

Page 216

4 We belong

Theme

A School Creed. Making a declaration aloud can help children to feel that they 'belong' to the family of school.

Let's talk

Who belongs to ... say – Beavers, Rainbow, Anchors, a church, etc?

Do you make any promises out loud when you join or soon after you join? What kind of promises?

We are going to say a verse that tells everyone that [Name of school] is *our* school and that we are making a promise to be good members of our school family.

The verse is called *A School Creed* and in it we make our promise aloud and altogether. Later, we shall learn this verse and repeat it often in our Assemblies.

(Teacher: This new 'Creed' is an alternative version of the school creeds found in the Assembly Books *Many Hearts* (1995) and *See, Another Day* (1997). Both creeds are printed in Appendix 1 on page 224 of this book and musical accompaniments to both creeds in Appendix 2. If you decide to adopt this creed, it is best learnt by traditional rote method. The simplest way for the children to learn the verse is to ask them to repeat each line aloud after you. Repeat the verse frequently and arrange for it be followed up in classroom time, as and when teachers are able.

A School Creed

This is our school
And we are family.
Let us promise together
That this shall be a place
Where we love one another
As brothers and sisters.
Let us promise together
That this shall be a happy place,
Where we can learn
About the world around us.

Songs to sing

Working together	*Every Colour* 37
Love somebody	*Tinderbox* 16
I belong to a family	*Sing it in the Morning* 3
Thank you for my friends	*Tinderbox* 31

No 'Thinking Time' is suggested for this assembly.

5 We're here to help

Theme

Asking adults for help.

Grown-ups are in school to help children. For a variety of reasons, children of all ages are often reluctant to ask teacher or an auxiliary to help them with a task or even something as basic as dressing. At the same time, they should realise that they cannot always obtain assistance immediately.

Let's talk

If you can't tie your shoe, what should you do?

If you can't read a word, what should you do? (*For both of these questions, the response should include the word 'try' somewhere in it.*)

You have tried for ten minutes to work out a sum and you still can't do it. What should you do next?

Time to listen

It is not a good idea to begin a job if you don't know how to do it properly. Sandy Squirrel soon found this out …

Sandy Squirrel and a Lot of Yellow Paint

'Whatever are you doing, Sandy?' asked Howard Hare, wandering through the front door of Acorn Cottage.

Sandy Squirrel was gazing up at his living-room ceiling murmuring, 'Uh-huh' and 'Aa-hah!', while in his hand was a large paint brush. On the floor by his feet was a large can of yellow paint. Howard coughed loudly, and Sandy seemed to come out of his daze with a little jump.

'Oh, hallo, Howard,' he squeaked, 'How long have you been there? Do you know, I have decided to paint the whole of my house a sunny, yellow colour.'

His hare friend looked worried. He knew what Sandy was like once he got an idea into his head.

'Hang on, Sandy, lad,' he said, quite agitated, 'You've never done painting before? Wouldn't it be quicker if we share the work?'

Howard was surprised by what happened next.

Sandy shouted angrily, 'Do you think I can't do *anything* by myself! Go, on, clear off and leave me alone!' Howard, amazed because Sandy Squirrel was never rude, left without another word.

A whole week later, as Howard passed Acorn Cottage on his way to Leafywoods Supermarket, he heard the sound of sobbing. The friendly hare tapped on the cottage door. It was opened by a sad and tearful Squirrel, covered from nose to bushy tail in yellow paint.

Howard Hare had never seen a yellow squirrel before. Two fat tears trickled through the paint down Sandy's furry yellow cheeks.

'Oh, my friend, I am so glad to see you,' whimpered the miserable animal, 'I was about to phone you to ask for your help. It all seemed so easy when I have seen you painting your house, but somehow it's all gone wrong. Instead of being so proud I should have accepted your help when it was offered to me.'

Howard nodded and said soothingly, 'Sandy, old pal, you need not be ashamed to asking for help, especially from me. Now, don't worry, we shall soon clean up all this mess and everything will look spick and span and bright and cheerful in no time. And yellow! As for you – into the bath, straight away!' I am pleased to tell you that is exactly what happened and that Sandy was soon a very happy squirrel, all bright-eyed and bushy-tailed.

The message is

If you don't know how to do a job – ask someone who does know.

Share your thoughts with everyone

Why do we usually ask grown-ups for help?

Should we only ever ask grown-ups for help?

Can other children help us?

Can you ask for help too often?

Think quietly about

Whether you would rather struggle with a problem rather than ask for help.

Whether it is silly not to ask for help if you need it.

Whether you can help other people at any time.

Songs to sing

With a little help from my friends	*Alleluya* 38
We will take care of you	*Every Colour* 36
Take care of a friend	*Every Colour* 35
Would you turn your back?	*Every Colour* 34
Side by side	*Ta-ra-ra-boom-de-ay* 36
Helping Grandma Jones	*Tinderbox* 27

Prayers

Page 216

6 Everybody tastes the same!

Theme

Racial attitudes

Let's talk

Few children at Key Stage 1 have any problems with racial differences and most schools have any potential difficulties well catered for. At the same time, it is worth encouraging children to think about the similarities in people regardless of background.

In what ways are you different from me?

In what ways are you different from the boy or girl standing/sitting next to you?

Time to listen

I expect most of you know what jelly babies are. This is a story about four of them. It is called:

Mollie and her Favourite Sweets

Mollie emptied out the four jelly babies she had left on to the table. The four sweets were different colours – green, orange, purple and red, and she was looking forward to eating them because Mollie just *loved* jelly babies.

'Now,' said Mollie to herself, 'Which one shall I eat first? I don't know which colour tastes the nicest. I think …'

She was interrupted by a little sweetie voice which said, 'Oh, you *must* eat me first, I taste *far* better than the others.' Mollie could not believe her ears. Well, would you if a jelly baby was talking to *you*?

'Did you say something to me, jelly baby? said Mollie.

'Oh, yes, indeed,' said Green Jelly Baby, cheerily, 'I said that green jelly babies are by far the most delicious flavour.'

Then Orange Jelly Baby sat up, shook off the sugar-dust that covered it and growled, 'No, they are aren't. No jelly baby has a flavour as lovely as orange ones. You do think a lot of yourself, Green, you really do. Eat me first, girl.'

Somehow, Mollie was not surprised when the purple jelly-baby and the red jelly baby stood up and started shouting, 'I am the best flavour and, then, in turn, 'Red!' 'Purple!' 'Red!' 'Purple!' 'Me first, me first!'

Then all four jelly babies started yelling at once and Mollie shrieked, 'Oh, do be quiet, you stupid little sweets. I tell you what I shall do – I shall bite off each of your heads in turn and then I shall eat the rest of the jelly baby whose head tastes the best.'

There was a chorus of horrified screams from the jelly babies 'You can't do … How dare you … What a wicked … Fancy biting off heads – Oo, you are awful … until Mollie bawled, 'OK, OK! I shan't do that. But do you know what I *shall do*?'

But, before any of the jelly-babies could answer, Mollie had gobbled the lot, one after the other, without looking at the colour. And, do you know, they all tasted exactly the same.

The message is

Jelly babies and people often look different but they are not so different, really

Share your thoughts with everyone

In what ways are you *like* everyone else?

Would you like to be someone else?

Why? Or why not?

Think quietly about

Why we should not regard ourselves as being better, in any way, than a person who is different from us.

Songs to sing

Sing a rainbow	*Apusskidu* 4
My ship sailed from China	*Apusskidu* 7
Brown girl in the ring	*Mango Spice* 38
Wind blows mangoes (Bengali song)	*Music Box Song Book* 57
We want to sing	*Sing a Silver Lining* 7
Consider yourself at home	*Sing a Silver Lining* 16
Side by side	*Ta-ra-ra boom-de-ay* 36

Prayers

Page 216

7 Some like to be different

Theme

Being different from others can be a good thing.

We tend to concentrate on the ways in which human beings resemble one another, but we should also remember that it is individual difference that makes for the diversity of humanity – and we should be glad of it, provided it does not engender discord and inequality. In other words, 'Vive la difference!'

Let's talk

I am different from you. Why?

Would you like to be me?

How are you different from your best friend?

Do you like being different from your best friend?

Why?

Time to listen

Wouldn't it be boring if everybody had the same toys? In this story, one toy is different from the others and it is easy to see why.

Toys Like Us!

'Look at me! Aren't I clever?' cried Spaceship, rolling across the toyshop floor with its green lights flashing.

Red Robot waggled its ray-gun up and down and and buzzed, 'Toys like us are the greatest!'

Then all the electric toys joined in – Police Car sounded its sirens, Jetplane flashed red lights, Monkey played a tune on its piano and Dinosaur stamped its plastic feet and roared. Dumper Truck went backwards and forwards and Clown spun a coloured ball. And all of them, as they performed their tricks, chanted, 'Batteries, batteries, Make us go, batteries, batteries, ho ho ho!'

All, that is, except little Red Fire Engine which had no batteries to make it work. It did not scuttle around, sound a siren, flash lights nor play a tune. It just sat on its four little white wheels and did – nothing.

Robot glared at the little vehicle and sneered, 'Hey, useless, don't you wish you had batteries to make you work like we do?'

'Yeah, you should get out of this toyshop,' growled Spaceship, 'How do you expect kids to play with a boring thing like you? You can't make a noise or flash your lights or do *anything* by yourself. You can't even move unless someone gives you a push. You're a useless toy.'

The other toys made a ring around Red Fire Engine, flashing lights and making a dreadul din. They started to bump into Red Fire Engine who took absolutely no notice of their silly antics.

Then Monkey said, 'I don't feel very well.' His arms stopped moving and the piano went quiet. And, one by one, all the toys stopped working until only Robot was left.

'I know what you are going to say, Red Fire Engine,' said Robot, 'We are no use when our batteries have run out. But I think you would like to be like us, all the same.'

Red Fire Engine said nothing. Because, of course, it knew that children could play with it at any time and make up their own games, too and that made it different from the rest of the toys.

And, so far as I know, that is exactly how the quiet little toy liked it.

Robot made a whirring noise as if it was going to speak again. But it did not. It could not. Its battery had run out.

The message is

Sometimes, it's good to be different from other people.

Share your thoughts with everyone

In what way are some children different from others?

Should we be unkind to children or grown-ups who like different things from the rest of us?

Think quietly about

Those children or grown-ups who are different from others because they cannot help it.

Doing our best to be kind to children or grown-ups who do not want to be different, but are, because they can do nothing about it.

Songs to sing

Guess how I feel	*Come & Praise* 89
Stick on a smile	*Every Colour* 43
Points of view	*Every Colour* 45
Why does it have to be me	*Music Box Song Book* 31 and *Tinderbox* 53
Loneliness	*Sing it in the Morning* 2
Can anyone tell me that?	*Tinderbox* 6

Prayers

Page 216

JUST YOU

8 Happy Birthday!

Theme

When *is* your birthday?

All children in Reception Year and beyond should know when their birthdays fall, but this is not always so.

Let's talk

Who can tell me when their birthday is (limitation needed!)?

What does a 'birthday' mean?

Why do you think children (and grown-ups) have birthday parties and presents?

Time to listen

You might feel sorry for the little boy in this story which is called:

Sam's Amazing Birthday Party

Sam rushed into the kitchen, panting, 'Mum, Mum, at my party this afternooon … can I have a kunj … a kunj … a magic man doing tricks like Tristan had at his party, can I, can I, can I?' Sam's mother looked at her son in dismay.

'But, darling, we are having Mr Jolly's puppet show. And where would I get a magician who would come at three hours' notice?'

Sam began to roar, 'WANNA MAGIC MAN WANNA MAGIC MAN WANNA …!' Then the doorbell rang and Mrs Osborne escaped from the noise. To her amazement, a plump little man, holding a bright blue suitcase, was standing at the door, grinning. He wore a bright blue suit and a bright blue top hat.

'Afternoon, lady,' he chattered, 'I believe you have a birthday party here today? Marvo the Magician, at your service. Kiddies amused, grown-ups amazed. Shall I come in?'

Before Mrs Osborne could say another word, Marvo had gone into the living room and shut the door. It was all very odd, especially when Mrs Osborne rang Mr Jolly, the puppeteer, to ask if he would cancel his visit and his wife said that he was ill and could not come, anyway. Sam could not believe his luck. Mrs Osborne did not know what to believe.

At half-past two the guests began to arrive at the party. Tristan handed over his present and sneered to Sam, 'I bet you haven't got a magician like I had at *my* party.'

'Well, that's where you're wrong. You'll see,' replied Sam, with a beaming smile on his freckled face.

'Can we have the magic show before we eat?' Sam asked his mother. Before she could answer, the guests, with Sam leading the way, trooped into the living room and sat down on the floor.

Marvo the magician laughed loudly and chortled, 'Hello, kiddies! Welcome to my amazing magic show!'

He waved his blue magic wand above a huge, bright blue top hat and warbled, 'Shoes and socks and smelly feet, now get ready for my treat! Alacazam ... Alacazoo ... silly sausage, skin of blue!' There was a bang, a bright blue flash and he threw his huge, bright blue top hat on to the carpet. Then, out of the hat, popped one bright blue rabbit, then another bright blue rabbit, then another and another and another and ... in no time at all there were *hundreds* of them.

They were *everywhere* – on the settee, on the chairs and ... on the party table. They ate every sausage, they ate every pizza, they ate every crisp, they ate *everything*. Even the magnificent chocolate birthday cake with seven candles on it. And the candles. There were so many rabbits that nobody could do a thing about it.

Then there came another bang and a bright blue flash and the whole room filled with blue smoke.

When the smoke cleared, the frightened children saw that the rabbits had disappeared. So had the top hat. So had Marvo the magician.

Nobody could explain what had happened at Sam's amazing birthday party, not even the police. Perhaps you can explain it? I can't.

The message is

Would you like your birthday party to be as exciting as Sam's?

Share your thoughts with everyone

How do you think Sam felt?

Should Tristan have been so rude?

Think quietly about

* Those children who never have birthday parties

or

How you should behave when invited to a birthday party.

Songs to sing

Growing	*Play School Song Book* 5
It's your birthday	*Sing a Song of Celebration* 50
New things to do	*Tinderbox* 58
Birthday song	*Tinderbox* 59
One, two, three	*Tinderbox* 65

Prayers

Page 217

9 How old?

Theme

Another view of birthdays. Children should know their ages!

The success of this assembly relies heavily on one or more children in the audience knowing about Leap Years and the extra day in February, so prepare your ground before hand. Of course, you might have a child who actually has a birthday on February 29 and this should make it easier.

Assuming you are not going to opt out of taking this assembly, it should, like all those in this section, be followed up during classroom time.

Let's talk

Who can tell me how old they are – in months *and* years?

What is a Leap Year?

Does anyone have a birthday on February 29th? (say no more!)

Time to listen

I am sure that children in your school would never behave like the two girls in this story!

And How Old are *You*?

'Good morning, children,' said Mrs Pringle brightly to the children in the school hall, 'and whose birthday is it today?' Four hands went up.

'Ah, Joseph,' said the headteacher, pointing to a little boy, 'and how old are you, then? Are you going to have a birthday party?'

Joseph gabbled away without taking breath, 'I'm going to the Zoo instead of having a birthday party and I am six today.' Two girls with hands up said they were seven and both of them were going to have birthday parties on Saturday.

Myrtle Mintoe announced that twenty children were coming to her party and she was going to have a *huge* cake and she was having a red bicycle for her birthday and she knew because she had seen it in her dad's shed.

'Oo!' squealed Abby loudly, 'You never! You aren't having a bicycle for your birthday and you are going to the pizza parlour for your birthday and there's only you and three other kids going. Your brother told me so. You're a fibber, Myrtle Mintoe!' Then Myrtle screamed at Abby and smacked her and Abby pinched Myrtle and the next thing was that Miss Pushem was marching the two of them out of the hall, howling.

When the children had settled down again, Mrs Grindle, looking very cross, asked Graham Peachey, who had his hand up, how old he was.

'I'm *one*, Mrs Grindle,' said Graham, grinning. Mrs Grindle became very angry. She left her chair, stood in front of him and wagged her finger in front of his nose.

'Graham Peachey! You are either stupid or you are being very, very rude. What are you talking about? How can you have had only one birthday? You are at least seven years old.'

Graham scowled and said, loudly, 'Because I was born on February 29th. And there's only been *one* February 29th since I was born! So I've only had *one* birthday, really!'

I won't tell you what Mrs Grindle said …

The message is

Best left until the children get back to their teaching areas where someone will work it out.

Share your thoughts with everyone

Who is the oldest person you know?

Can you tell us in which year they were born?

What year is it now?

'Quiet thinking' is not useful for this assembly.

Songs to sing

Any of the songs suggested for Assembly 8 and

Birthday round	*Harlequin* 42
Each day different	*Harlequin* 43
Maja pade – Let's all be happy	*Tinderbox* 57

Prayers

Page 217

10 Home, sweet home

Theme

Ensuring that all children know their home addresses.

This assembly aims to remind children that it is important to know home and school addresses.

Let's talk

Your address is where you live.

Who can tell me their address? (*Some children will offer district, county, postcode, et al, whereas a few will not know their correct address, or any part of it. Many children will include the country and the world, in their address. You can make of that what you will.*)

Time to listen

This story tells what happened to Dilly Dimple who had forgotten where she lived.

Dilly Dimple and a Bicycle Ride

When Dilly Dimple was four years old, she could have told you that she lived at '2 Rose Lane, Dandydell and it is a house with a red roof and a green front door.' Then, one day, all the Dimple's furniture was loaded into a big van and the Dimple family moved to a brand new house in another town.

Dilly liked the new house and made up her mind to learn the new address which was '6 Nutty Close, Tubbywick', but she was so busy arranging her bedroom that she never seemed to have the time. She did learn, '6 Nutty Something or other' but that was all, although she *did* learn her telephone number.

One day, Dilly set off for a ride without telling anyone. As she cycled along, she saw a rainbow and went to look for the end of it and she cycled for what seemed like hours. Then, oh, dear, the rainbow disappeared. So she sat on a grassy bank and made a daisy chain instead.

But when the little girl set off for home, she had no idea how to get there or what the address was. All she could remember was '6 Nutty somewhere or other'. Which was not much use. Then along came a postman, whose name I think was Pat, driving a bright red van.

'What's the matter?' he said to Dilly, most kindly.

Dilly said, in a lost little voice, 'Please, Mr Postman, I'm Dilly Dimple and I can't find my way home and I live at 6 Nutty somewhere or other ... no I don't and it has a green roof and a tall door, no it doesn't, oh dear, it has a tall roof and a red door, no, it doesn't, oh dear, I *am* lost and I don't know what to do but my phone number is 01333 109876,' and she began to cry.

Don't worry,' said the postman, taking out his mobile phone and ringing Mrs Dimple.

She soon came to fetch Dilly in her car. She was a little bit cross with her daughter but she made sure that Dilly learned two things that day. One was to remember her new address and the other was not to go off on bicycle rides on her own – especially when she was only a little person. But you already know those, don't you?

The message is

You should always know your home address and your telephone number if possible. And you should never go off on your own without telling someone.

Share your thoughts with everybody

What is the address of this school?

Why should you know the name of your school?

Think quietly about

Being lost and not being able to remember the address of your home.

Going out, and how worried your family would be if they did not know where you had gone.

Not having an address at all.

Songs to sing

The building song	*Come & Praise* 61
I have a tiny little house	*Music Box Song Book* 86
In a cottage in a wood	*Okki-tokki-unga* 24
At half past three we go home to tea	*Someone's Singing, Lord* 58
Place to be	*Tinderbox* 34
Welcome home	*Tinderbox* 60

Prayers

Page 217

11 Be healthy, be wise

Theme

Encouraging children to go to bed at a sensible time, because adequate sleep is important.

Children are expert at avoiding going to bed so, if teachers can help a little towards persuading them that they are doing themselves no favours, it has to be time well spent.

Let's talk

Who goes to bed when they are told?

Who tries to get out of going to bed when they are told?

Why?

Time to listen

Meet the animals in the Beautiful Garden. Perhaps you can feel sorry for Giraffe?

The Tired Giraffe

Long ago, all the animals in the world lived in a special place called the Beautiful Garden. The only human who lived there to look after the animals was called The Keeper.

One animal was Giraffe. Nowadays, all giraffes in the world are marked all over with light brown patches. But Giraffe in our tale had a pretty, cream-coloured coat, as soft as a butterfly's wing.

Giraffe spent a lot of time staring at the stars, often staying awake all night.

'Keeper?' she said, 'What are the bright lights that shine in the sky? Will they ever fall on us in the Garden?' The Keeper told her that she should be sleeping at night, not worrying about the stars, or she would never grow up. Then, one hot day, she was so tired that she fell asleep in the shade of a tontow tree, which has only a few large leaves on each of its branches.

Sunlight streamed down between the leaves, falling on to her soft coat and making bright, warm patches, but Giraffe slept on. As she slept, the parts of her cream-coloured fur on which the sunlight was falling turned, little by little, to a pale brown colour instead of cream.

Gorilla tried to wake her, but Giraffe slept too soundly and the patches grew darker and darker. To her dismay, when she woke, she found that her pretty, cream-coloured coat was covered all over in pale brown patches.

When Giraffe saw what had happened, she wept bitterly but The Keeper told her that it would do her no good. What was done was done. Her coat would be like that for ever and so would that of all giraffes that came after her. And all because she would not go to sleep at the proper time.

I wish I could tell you that Giraffe learnt her lesson. Oh dear, no. All she learnt was never to fall asleep in the sun again. And she never did find out what the stars really are.

The message is

It is important for children of your age to get plenty of sleep and not to argue about going to bed at a sensible time.

Share your thoughts with everyone

What is the right time to go to bed on school days? Why?

What happens if children stay up late every night?

Think quietly about

People who work at night.

People who have no bed in which to sleep.

Songs to sing

Morningtown ride	*Apusskidu* 25
Hay ho! Time to go to bed	*Flying a Round* 14
I jump out of bed in the morning	*Okki-tokki-unga* 47
Lazy coconut tree	*Ta-ra-ra boom-de-ay* 18
Laura the big giraffe	*The Multi-coloured Music Bus* 28

Prayers

Page 217

12 Eat healthy, eat wise

Theme

Encouraging children to vary their diet.

Not all teachers consider that children's eating habits are their concern and some parents will not think so either, but there is nothing to lose if we try to point children in the right nutritional direction.

Let's talk

Some schools have discontinued school meals as a matter of financial policy, so the first three questions may not be relevant.

Who has school meals/dinners/lunches?

Who enjoys them? All of them?

What do you think about them?(Limit comments!)

What foods are good for us?

What foods are not good for us?

Are foods like that always bad for us?

Time to listen

Do you remember Bobkin Brockle and his visit to the Big Boss Brockle? This story is about another of his bad habits and is called:

Moomy Mushrooms

One Brockly springtime, Bobkin Bumble started to get strange ideas about food. All he would eat were bright blue Moomy mushrooms which taste much better than they look. Especially if you are a Brockle.

'I do wish you would try eating some dandelion porridge,' groaned his Mum at breakfast one day, 'or some spider sausages. Moomy mushrooms for breakfast, dinner, tea and supper. They can't be good for you.' 'One of these days you will turn as blue as the mushrooms are, see if you don't.'

Bobkin grunted, 'Yik. Don't like them. Shan't ever eat anything else, only Moomy mushrooms.'

And for ages, that was all he ate. Then, one bouncy, Brockly morning, Bobkin woke up and shuffled to the bathroom where he looked in the mirror, wiggling his long, pointed ears and scratching his tufty hair, as he woke up very, very slowly.

But he soon woke up when he realised that he was wiggling long, pointed *bright blue* ears and scratching tufty, *bright blue hair*! In fact, he was blue *all over*!

As you might expect, Bobkin ran screeching to his Mum, expecting to be cuddled and comforted, but all she said was 'I told you so.' And Bobkin had to go to school like that for weeks and weeks. You can imagine how much he was teased by the other Brockle children, which was very unkind of them.

Snow was on the ground before he stopped being blue. In the meantime, Bobkin tried other foods and, to his surprise, he found that he *did* like things other than Moomy mushrooms.

Not that he ever said that he did.

The message is

Don't say that you dislike a food before you have tasted it for yourself.

Share your thoughts with everyone

(**Be aware of children who may have weight problems*)

What does this story tell us about food and eating?

Can anyone tell us why some foods are bad for us?

Think quietly about

How fortunate we are to have plenty of food to eat.

People who do not have enough to eat.

Songs to sing

Super-supper march	*Apusskidu* 6
Paintbox	*Harlequin* 32
Pease pudding hot	*Music Box Song Book* 54
Magical food	*Music Box Song Book* 59
Eat brown bread	*Okki-tokki-unga* 9
Mairzy doats and doazy doats	*Ta-ra-ra-boom-de-ay* 24

Prayers

Page 217

13 Terrific Teeth

Theme

Taking care of one's teeth.

Let's talk

Who has some teeth missing?

Where have they gone?

Did you put any of those teeth under your pillow?

Did anything happen?

Time to listen

The tooth fairy in this story is a bit unusual:

Who'd be a Tooth Fairy?

Katrina was a bit surprised when she woke up and saw Tarquin sitting on the end of her bed. He was no bigger than her smallest teddy bear and he looked extremely miserable.

'Hello,' said Katrina. 'Are you a fairy? You look too grumpy to be one even if you are dressed like one.'

The visitor groaned. 'I'm not a flippin' fairy,' he growled, 'I'm a pixie. And a boy pixie at that.'

Katrina tried not to laugh. The pixie had big pointed ears, stubby little wings and a *very* dirty face. He was wearing a silver dress with a frilly skirt like a ballet tutu, and on his scrubby hair was a silver head band. Besides that, he was carrying a wand which sparkled in the moonlight that was streaming through the window.

'Then why are you wearing a fairy frock?' giggled Katrina. 'You do look silly. And what are you doing in my bedroom, anyway?'

The pixie stood up and squeaked, 'I'm being a tooth fairy! The Fairy Queen said I had to or else she would turn me into a tube of toothpaste. All because Daisy, one of the proper tooth fairies for this town is off sick with toothache and Dinah, the other one, has got sparrow pox.'

'Don't you mean chicken pox?' said Katrina. The pixie sighed.

'Oh, you humans are stupid,' he snapped, 'fairies aren't big enough to have *chicken* pox. Anyway, I wouldn't mind doing the tooth fairy job, but *boy* pixies shouldn't be made to dress like this. I do know what I have to do, you know – take away a tooth that's come out of your mouth and leave a fifty pence coin in exchange.' Katrina looked surprised.

'But I haven't had a tooth come out for weeks,' she said, 'I have got one wobbly one, but are you sure you've got the right person?'

Tarquin looked annoyed. He took a scrap of paper out of the bag on his belt and read, 'Miranda Parry, aged seven, of 15 Appletree Close,' he snapped. 'That's you, isn't it?'

Katrina said, no, she was Katrina Merry, aged six, who lived at 15 Peartree Road and she had no idea where Appletree Close was.

The pixie sighed, 'Oh, I'll never find my way round this town. I must say I'm fed up with this. I think I'd rather be a tube of toothpaste. Goodbye, girl.' And he fluttered off through the open window, grumbling as he went.

The message is

There isn't one, really – it's just to get you thinking about teeth.

Share your thoughts with everyone

Who likes going to the dentist? Tell us why.

Why is it important to visit a dentist at all?

No 'Quiet thinking' is suggested for this topic.

Songs to sing

Pairs	*Play School Song Book* 4
Growing	*Play School Song Book* 5
Snappity snappity crocodile	*Multi-coloured Music Bus* 34
The shark, the tiger and the crocodile	*Sing it in the Morning* 50
You can do it	*Sing a Silver Lining* 9
I've got a body	*Tinderbox* 5

Prayers

Page 217

*14 Something in the air

Theme

Encouraging children to keep themselves clean.

Children usually arrive at school shiny and well-scrubbed (we can do little about those who do not) and they should be encouraged to remain reasonably wholesome at the end of the day. This informal approach to the subject of cleanliness may be developed at classroom level to encourage good practice in hygiene, such as hand-washing at appropriate times. The more serious matter of children who have genuine hygiene problems is for other times and other places.

Let's talk

Which do you prefer, baths or showers?

Tell us about it.

Time to listen

Children should not need to be told to keep themselves clean but they can be just as lazy as the baby hippo in this story.

Mud, Glorious Mud

Hoofa is a baby hippopotamus who loves wallowing about in thick, black, oozy, squelchy, smelly mud. And, if you went walkabout any day along the edge of the river you would have seen him and the rest of the herd all enjoying a lovely, squishy, squashy wallow in the thick, black, oozy, squelchy mud which gets smellier and smellier as the scorching afternoon drifts by.

Then, as evening fell and the sun became a huge red ball, you would have heard the lively noise of splashing and snorting as all the hippos rushed into the river to wash off the mud that had made a thick crust on their tough skins and kept them cool through the day.

Except Hoofa. He did not like getting wet. His mother tried pushing

Hoofa into the water with her big, blunt snout, but he always ran away and hid behind a tree. So, when all the newly-washed and sweet-clean hippos went back to their cool, long grass to sleep, just one small hippo was still covered with a thick coat of dry, smelly mud – Hoofa.

Every day, his coat of mud got thicker and thicker and he got smellier and smellier. Soon, the smell became so bad that no one would play with Hoofa nor sleep near him.

Puzzled, Hoofa asked his mother, 'Why don't the other little hippos want to play with me or sleep near me?' Mrs Hippo told Hoofa that it was because of the awful smell that followed him wherever he went.

'But *why* do I smell awful?' asked the little hippo.

'Because, child,' said Honka, gently, 'you won't wash off the thick, dry mud that is stuck to you, and it smells awful.' Which made Hoofa feel ashamed and, the very next day, he took an evening dip with the rest of the herd and really enjoyed splashing about in the water. And, of course, he was never smelly again.

The message is

Washing and bathing or showering regularly is very important.

* *Share your thoughts with everyone*

What has a hippo to do with children?

Think quietly about:

People who find it hard to have a bath or a shower because they have an illness of some kind.

*People who have no bath or shower in their homes.

Large families who have to take their turn to use the bath or shower.

What really *can* happen if people do not bath or shower as often as they should?

Songs to sing

The hippopotamus song	*Apusskidu* 40
Water of life	*Come & Praise* 3
Because you care	*Every Colour* 31

Podge the hippopotamus — *Multi-coloured Music Bus* 30
Sing a song of people — *Tinderbox* 18
The gift of water — *Sing it in the Morning* 53

Prayers

Page 217

15 Play Safe 1

Theme

Playing safely.

Children are not always conscious of danger when they are playing. There are many hazards that can cause accidents – watery, derelict, industrial and agricultural and, as we all know, traffic.

Let's talk

Tell me about some places where you play after school.

Do you play on a busy road?

Do you play near a pond or a lake or a river?

Do the grown-ups who look after you know where you are playing?

If not, what would they do if they found out?

Time to listen

I hope you will be more sensible than the hens in this story!

The Foolish Hens

Speckly Brown Hen clucked to her friend, 'Come on, Spotty, don't be such a scaredy scrag. Let's go up to the Curly Cabbage Field and chase the caterpillars.' 'I am bored with this old Scratch-Patch.' Just then, along came Clarence Cockerel, Captain of the Scratch-Patch.'

'I heard that, oh, I heard that,' he cackled, 'Let me tell you that nobody in *my* Scratch-Patch goes into the Curly Cabbage Field. It is much too risky, much too risky.'

Spotty Brown Hen squawked, 'Why not? We could have a lot of fun up there.'

The big rooster puffed his feathers, shook his bright red comb and crowed, 'Just you stay here where you are safe, where you are safe, little hens. The Curly Cabbage Field is not a safe place to play. I have spoken.'

Spotty Brown Hen waited until Clarence had gone and cackled, 'Take no notice of that old Captain. Let's go and play in the Curly Cabbage Field.' In as much time as it takes to shake a feather duster, the two little hens had chicken-trotted to the Curly Cabbage Field, which was full of tall curly cabbages, called curly kale.

They had a great time, but after a while the two little hens began to get tired of caterpillar-annoying. I suppose it was because the caterpillars could not answer back.

'I think we had better make our way home,' clucked Speckly Brown Hen. 'It will soon be dark. Oo, what was that?' The little brown hen thought she had heard a snigger behind one of the tall curly cabbages.

Then … she saw one foxy-whiskered face peeping out from behind the curly cabbage plant, then another foxy-whiskered face peeping out from behind a different curly cabbage plant, then another, and another, and another.

The frightened Speckly Brown Hen screeched to the Spotty Brown 'Yah! Foxes! Quick, let's get out of here!'

The two little hens turned tail and crashed out of the Curly Cabbage Patch, pelted through the Potato Patch and scrambled through the Strawberry Patch until they could scrabble and squeeze through the fence of the Scratch-Patch, where they fell on the ground, chicken-panting and chicken-puffing.

Next day, Speckly Brown Hen said to Spotty Brown Hen, as they pecked at their morning corn, 'Curly Cabbage Fields and foxes are not good news for chickens. In future we will stay and play where we are safe. Even if we are bored. Won't we?' Which was a very wise thing to say and do.

The message is:

Always find somewhere safe to play.

Share your thoughts with everyone

Tell us about some places that are *not* safe to play.

Tell us about some places that *are* safe to play.

If you play somewhere that is not safe, what might happen?

Think quietly about

The trouble you could cause by playing in unsafe places.

The danger you might bring to other people by playing in unsafe places.

Whether it is selfish to play in unsafe places.

Songs to sing

Look around	*Every Colour* 9
Use your eyes	*Every Colour* 11
We will take care of you	*Every Colour* 36
Messing about on the river	*Jolly Herring* 72
I went to the cabbages	*Tinderbox* 46
New things to do	*Tinderbox* 58

Prayers

Page 217

*16 Play safe 2

Theme

Never go off with strangers …

It has long been obvious that teachers must be careful to strike a balance with this topic – we do not want to discourage children from relating to strangers entirely but, at the same time, caution has to be exercised. The local police liaison officers will usually visit to talk on this subject.

Let's talk

Best left, until it is 'Time to think'.

Time to listen

The stranger in this story meant well and we should learn from it.

Marigold and a Stranger

'I can't open this stupid nut,' said a little voice. Marigold, aged seven, stopped walking and and saw a tiny figure sitting on a twig and holding a fat hazel nut which was almost as big as herself.

'You're a fairy!' gasped Marigold, looking at the tiny creature dressed all in green. A pair of shiny wings, like a dragonfly's, grew out of her back.

'Of course I'm a fairy and my name is Ariadne,' snapped the tiny person. 'Please will you going to open this nut for me?' Marigold took the nut and cracked it with her teeth, which was not a clever thing to do.

Ariadne ate most of the nut and then said, 'Thank you. That was kind of you. Now come and see where I live. Not many humans get to see a fairy's home. Follow the dancing sunbeam – that will be me.'

Sure enough, a sunbeam appeared and led the way.

Deep in the green shade of the woods, the sunbeam disappeared and there was Ariadne, sitting on a fallen tree trunk.

'Marigold,' said the fairy, 'does anyone know where you are?' The little girl gasped. No one *did* know where she was.

'That was foolish of you,' laughed Ariadne, 'You should *never* go off with anyone you don't know, whatever they tell you. Haven't you been told that before?'

'But you're not a stranger,' laughed Marigold, 'You're a fairy!'

The fairy waved her sparkling silver wand. Woosh! Instead of a pretty fairy, an ugly old witch stood in front of her, cackling. Then she waved *her* twisted old green wand. Woosh! The witch vanished and Ariadne, the fairy, was back, sitting on the tree trunk once more and smiling.

'You see, you silly little human,' said Ariadne, 'I *am* a fairy. But I could have been *anybody*. Couldn't I?' But before Marigold could answer, the fairy vanished again – and Marigold woke up. She was in her own little bed at home – it had all been a dream.

But, after that she knew she would *never* go off with someone she did not know. And I'm sure you wouldn't, either. Would you?

The message is

You know what the message is!

Share your thoughts with everyone

If a stranger speaks to you, what should you do?

Responses will vary – play it by ear, according to what the children have to say.

Think quietly about

Promising *yourself* that you will always be careful if a stranger talks to you.

Songs to sing

I whistle a happpy tune	*Apusskidu* 3
Use your eyes	*Every Colour* 11
Do your best	*Every Colour* 48
Oh, Mr Policeman	*Silly Aunt Sally* 64
Sing a song of people	*Tinderbox* 18
Don't you push me down	*Tinderbox* 26

Prayers

Page 217

17 Bed o'clock

Theme

The importance of learning to tell the time.

Let's talk

(*You will have to refer to a clock in the Assembly room*)

Hands up the children who can tell me what time it is now by the school clock.

Who can tell me the same time in another way? (looking for am/pm or 24-hour clock, depending on what answers you get)

Time to listen

I hope you don't say the time in the same way as Sam did in this story.

Strange Times!

'I'm coming,' called Mr Lenton, the village shopkeeper, 'I don't usually open until nine o'clock. Don't you know what time it is?' Yawning, he opened the door and saw Sam standing on the step.

Sam said, 'Oh, yes. It is breakfast o'clock!'

'That's a funny time,' said Mr Lenton, as he placed a carton of milk on the counter, 'What time is that, then?' Sam, aged five, looked at the shopkeeper as if he was a really stupid grown-up.

'The time I have my breakfast, of course,' he sniffed, 'It's time to go to school at school o'clock, time to go home at home o'clock and so on. See?'

Mr Lenton thought for a moment and said, 'But how do you *know* when it *is* school o'clock and home o'clock and – er – breakfast o'clock?'

Sam huffed and sighed, 'Someone always tells me, of course.'

Mr Lenton gave up and said, 'Why are you so early this morning?'

'Oh,' said Sam, excitedly, 'We have to be at the Delbury service station at coffee o'clock and we mustn't be late, because we catch the Eurostar at tea o'clock and we arrive in Disneyland, Paris, at bed o'clock.'

The shopkeeper could not help laughing. Sam glared at him and growled, 'Why are you laughing? There's nothing funny about going to Disneyland.'

'No, no,' said Mr Lenton, shaking his head, 'It's just that I find your way of telling the time rather amusing.'

Sam said sharply, 'Well, I think it's better than those silly old *numbers* times. I don't understand those. Not even on my Mickey Mouse watch.'

The shopkeeper grinned and said, kindly, 'Yes, Sam, *you* might understand your 'o'clocks' but nobody else can. People have different breakfast-times and coffee-times and bed-times but everybody can understand when it is six o'clock or ten o'clock because it is the same time for everybody.'

Sam scowled again. 'Humph,' he growled, 'Well, I think it's silly. My way is *much* better.' And off he went, muttering to himself.

Mind you, he spent a lot of time on the Eurostar train staring at his Mickey Mouse watch. After a while, he asked his Mum what the real time was when Micky's long arm pointed to the twelve and his short arm pointed to the three.

He asked a lot more questions about telling the time, too, after that. Do you think it was a good idea?

The message is

It is a good thing if you can tell the time *properly.*

'Share your thoughts' and 'Think quietly about' are omitted as the topic is part of everyday curricular activity.

Songs to sing

All night, all day	*Alleluya* 75
Time is a thing	*Come & Praise* 64
Song of the clock	*Tinderbox* 7
A time for everything	*Songs for every day* 25
My Grandfather's clock	*Ta-ra-ra-boom-de-ay* 54

Prayers

Page 217

18 Play Safe 3

Theme

Treating water with respect

Let's talk

Who can swim?

Where do you go to swim? (a real location)

How do we know if someone is able to swim *properly*?

Time to listen

Of course, ducks don't have to learn how to swim – or do they?

In this story, one little duck had problems.

Diddy's first Ducking

Diddy's six brothers and sisters had skin between their toes and their beaks were flatter than his. His mother, Dora, however, told herself that he was still her baby, and looks aren't everything, and at least their coats of fluffy yellow down looked alike.

Of course, Dora took as much care of him as she did the others and Diddy got his fair share of tadpoles and little fish and at night, too, he was tucked up under her wing as safely as the other ducklings.One morning, Dora announced that she was going to take all her children for their first swimming lesson. The seven excited little ones followed Mum down to the green pond.

Now,' said Dora, 'All you have to do is to do exactly as I do.' She waddled into the water, moved her flat feet backwards and forwards and – she was swimming! It looked easy.

The children toddled after her, in a line, into the cold water – one duckling – plop!, two ducklings – plop!, three, four, five, six, plop! plop! plop! plop! Then in went Diddy. But he didn't plop!

As soon as he touched the water he let out a terrified squawk and splashed frantically back to the bank. Dora heard his cry and swam back to ask what was the matter.

Diddy squeaked, 'Oo, it was horrible – all cold and wet and I felt myself sinking in the water!' Dora stroked him with her wing.

'Nonsense, little one,' she clucked, soothingly, 'You can't possibly sink. Ducks don't sink.'

'If they *are* ducks,' said a strange voice. Dora and Diddy looked round and saw a tatty old cockerel, sitting under a bush.

'Whatever do you mean?' quacked Dora.

'He's not a duck,' clucked the cockerel, 'Look at his feet and his beak. He's a *chicken*. And chickens don't like water.'

Dora thought about it and then realised – she couldn't remember laying seven eggs. So where had Diddy come from? Perhaps you can tell her? And me.

The message is

Learn to swim if at all possible.

Share your thoughts with everyone

Tell me why being able to swim could be important.

Tell me why learning to swim can be great fun.

Think quietly about

Making up your mind to learn to swim if you get the chance.

Songs to sing

Take me to the seaside	*Harlequin* 27
Six little ducks	*Okki-tokki-unga* 41
You can do it	*Sing a Silver Lining* 9
For all the strength we have	*Someone's Singing, Lord* 16
Hands to work and feet to run	*Someone's Singing, Lord* 21
I've got a body	*Tinderbox* 5

Prayers

Page 217

19 It's yours!

Theme

Taking care of personal possessions, at home and at school.

Children often seem to believe in the idea of 'Easy come, easy go', especially when they enjoy a lot of possessions and, consequently, are often careless about taking care of their property.

Let's talk

Who owns a bicycle? (or any other possession -computer, doll, 'Scalextric' set, etc)

What do you do with it when you have finished riding it?

Do you ever clean it?

How else do you look after it?

Time to listen

I hope you all treat your toys better than Nancy does in this story.

Nancy Doesn't Care

All the toys in the Old Toy Box woke with a start as Clive Clockwork Clown crashed into the box, squeaking and wheezing as he fell.

Mandy, the Glammy doll, opened her one eye and sat up. 'Who said you could come into this Toy Box?' she asked haughtily. 'We only allow toys that have been bashed and battered by Nasty Nancy, the dreadful girl who owns us.'

Before Clive could answer, Action Man, who had no arms, croaked, 'You don't look as if nasty Nancy had been taking out her temper on you. You don't look damaged at all to me. Do you know, that dreadful child pulled off my arms just because her Mum said she couldn't go to the cinema. It wasn't my fault.'

The Clockwork Clown tried to say something with his painted smile but Squishy Spider waved three legs and wailed, 'And that horrid child was not allowed to go to a party so she pulled off five of my legs. One at a time. Said it made her feel better. It didn't make *me* feel good, I can tell you. It would have hurt, too, if I'd been real.'

Sid Scooter rattled his only wheel and squeaked (he needed oiling), 'I don't see why Clown can't come in here. Nancy isn't the only child to damage toys, you know.'

Monty Teddy Bear, who only had one eye, one arm and one leg, growled, 'I think this clockwork clown is a spy. He isn't even bent. And he's got all his legs and arms and most of his paint. So what are you doing here, Clown?'

Clive said, in a strange, rusty voice, 'No I haven't been battered like you have. But Nasty Nancy left me outside in the garden for six whole months. It was jolly cold and wet out there but she didn't care. So I am just as broken as any of you are because I am all rusty and my clockwork doesn't work any more. Being left outside is just as bad as being pulled to bits. So there.'

Well, what could the rest of the broken toys do but let him stay?

Did I hear someone ask if this is a true story? Well, what do you think? But, if toys really could speak …

The message is

You should take care of things that are given to you.

Share your thoughts with everyone

Why do children break their own toys?

Have you ever broken a toy? Why?

Have you ever left a toy out of doors? Why?

Think quietly about

Having ever broken something in a fit of temper.

Whether you felt better afterwards.

Wishing you had not broken it and why.

Songs to sing

Don't you think we're lucky?	*Every Colour* 25
How do you feel today?	*Play School Song Book* 1
A time for everything	*Songs for Every Day* 25
The angry song	*Tinderbox* 9
Let's pretend	*Tinderbox* 25

Prayers

Page 217

FAMILY AND YOU

*20 Who matters most?

Theme

Priorities in a family.

Most children, probably up to the age of seven, regard themselves as being the centre of the universe. It would be unrealistic to think that the school can modify this attitude but we can at the very least begin to point children in the right direction.

This assembly might also contribute in another small way – children with newly-arrived siblings often exhibit anti-social behaviour or withdrawal attitudes in school, once they realise that they are no longer the sole centre of attention at home.

Let's talk

At home, do you:

Insist on watching the TV programmes that *you* want?

Expect everybody to eat only food that *you* like?

Expect to have *exactly* the Christmas or birthday present you want, regardless of how much it might cost?

Time to listen

Herbert has a Surprise

Herbert Hopskip of Daisy Warren was not a happy bunny. He had come home from school but where was Mum? She was always in when he got home from school.

He was hungry and his tummy rumbled. Then to his surprise his Auntie Bessie Bobtail, who lived next door, bustled in and put a big steaming plate of buttered parsnips on the table in front of Herbert.

She said cheerily, 'Come along, Herbert, eat up your supper and we shall go and see your Mummy and your five new sisters in Great Warren hospital.' Suddenly, Herbert didn't feel hungry any more.

'What five sisters?' he screeched, 'I haven't *got* any sisters!'

Auntie Bessie chortled, 'You have now, my boy.'

'But ... but ... but ... ' spluttered Herbert, 'What do I want *them* for? He began to cry and howl and stamp his feet.

'Now, now,' soothed Auntie Bessie, 'Think how lucky you are. Not many boy rabbits get the chance to help their Mummy with beautiful new babies like this, you know.'

Suddenly, Herbert howled, picked up his dinner and threw it into the fireplace. The plate smashed into smithereens and the parsnips splattered in all directions.

He jumped up and down and shrieked, 'I don't want five nasty babies in this burrow! I hate babies! And they're girls! Send them back!'

'What a dreadful thing to say,' said a shocked Auntie Bessie.

'No, it's not!' bawled Herbert, 'Who's gonna cook my dinners and wash my shirts and make my bed?'

'Oh, I see,' said Auntie Bessie, with a sniff, 'All you are thinking about is yourself. I'm afraid you will just have to get used to the idea that your dinners and your shirts and your bed are not as important as they used to be.'

'They are to me,' whimpered Herbert, 'I'm not big enough to look after myself.'

'Of course not,' said Auntie kindly, 'Nobody would expect a boy rabbit of your age to do that. Even if you are the big brother in the family we shall still look after you and love you just as much. It's just that you won't be any more important than the rest of the family.'

The message is

You are not the only person who matters in a family.

Share your thoughts with everyone

Do some children think they are the most important child in the school family? Why? (Avoid personalities!)

Think quietly about

Other people in your home or school family who might *need* looking after more than you do.

Songs to sing

Ruskin the Rabbit	*Alphabet Zoo Book* 52
What's it like in the place where you live?	*Play School Song Book* 14
I belong to a family	*Sing it in the Morning* 3
A time for everything	*Songs for Every Day* 25
Love somebody	*Tinderbox* 16
Why does it have to be me?	*Music Box Song Book* 31
	Tinderbox 53

Prayers

Page 218

21 Little words

Theme

The importance of a real 'Please' and 'Thank you'.

Children often need encouragement to say these words at the right time. If they do not need encouragement then this Assembly applauds their manners.

Let's talk

Tell me the correct way to ask if you can leave the room (or whatever euphemism is customary in your school).

Supposing you come across a hard word in a book that you cannot read. Tell me how you would ask someone else to help you.

If someone helps you to read the word, what should you say afterwards?

Time to listen

Her Ever-so-Highness Princess Splendid thought she was *so* important. That was no excuse for being rude.

Princess Splendid and a Wizard

Princess Splendid had been invited, along with all the Royal Family and their friends, to a party given by Wizard Stickler, who had been visiting the Court Wizard, Cleverclogs.

Wizard Stickler did not take long to get the party ready – all he had to do was to wave his magic wand a few times and, in two shakes of a black cat's tail, the table was full of goodies to eat.

The party had only been going for ten minutes and everyone enjoyed playing party games when Princess Splendid announced that because *she* was hungry, everybody could start to eat the party food.

The Wizard was annoyed, because it was *his* party and it should have been he who said it was time to eat. But, although he looked angry, he said nothing because he was a very polite Wizard.

He still said nothing when the guests lined up for their dishes of jelly and ice cream and the Princess pushed everybody out of the way so she could be first in line.

The Wizard did his best to smile politely at her as he spooned out a big dishful of the red, blue, green, yellow, black, purple and orange striped jelly which wobbled wonderfully and tasted tremendous, topped by some fantastic fizzy ice cream which tasted even better.

'There you are, Your Highness,' he chuckled, 'Now what do you say to old Wizard Stickler? Hm?'

The Princess glared at him and snapped, 'Is that all I get? Gimme some more, you old meany.'

'No, no, Princess,' said the Wizard, gently, 'I meant, *what* do you say when someone gives you something?'

Splendid glared at him and said icily, '*I* am a Princess. So *I* don't have to say anything.' Before she knew what had happened, she found she was standing *under* the party table looking at a mouse's nose. The mouse was as big as she was because the Princess had shrunk until she was no bigger than a toy soldier.

Grinning, the Wizard peeped under the table and asked, 'Have you remembered what you should say? You know, two special little words?'

The mouse said to the Princess, 'I think you had better remember those two words, otherwise you might disappear altogether.'

The Princess thought it might be a good idea, and said, sulkily, the important words she had known all the time – 'Thank you.' And, before she knew it, she was standing back in line again holding her dish and saying 'Thank you' again to a smiling Wizard Stickler.

Not only that, but every day after that party she always remembered to say 'Please' and 'Thank you.'

And now I have finished telling this story, what should you say to me?

The message is

People who give you something usually expect you to say 'Thank You' and it is also a good idea to say 'Please' when you want something.

Share your thoughts with everyone

Do you think it is a waste of time saying 'Please' and 'Thank you'? Why?

Are there any other things that people expect if they do something for you, but do not cost anything?

Think quietly about

Things done for you for which you should have said, 'Thank you' and did not.

Which is more important, saying 'Please' or 'Thank you'? Or are they both the same?

Songs to sing

Both sides now	*Alleluya* 33
One more step	*Come & Praise* 47
I can climb	*Every Colour* 17
Stick on a smile	*Every Colour* 43
Sing a song of people	*Tinderbox* 18
Because you care	*Tinderbox* 31

Prayers

Page 218

*22 Chopsticks, forks and fingers

Theme

Eating politely.

Different cultures have different table manners. Acceptable table behaviour varies a great deal but there are certain norms in all cultures as regards eating and drinking and it is worth reminding children that certain standards are expected, at least at school – for example, not all food is 'finger-food' and not everyone wishes to see another person's back teeth when chewing or to hear the intake of liquids.

Let's talk

Who enjoys watching other children eating? Why? (No names!)

Who thinks they do not offend other children (or adults) when they eat? Why?

Time to listen

People in different parts of the world have different ideas about table manners. Who has the better manners in this story?

Gabby's Cousins

Gabby was very excited. His cousins from far-away Hicktown were coming to stay and he had never met them before. When the boy and girl arrived, they seemed like anybody else, apart from their strange yellow hats and yellow scarves. They soon unpacked, washed their hands, and sat at the table, ready for dinner.

Gabby's Mum brought in a big bowl of chicken-and-dumpling stew and ladled a big helping into each of the children's dishes.

Gabby picked up some stew on his spoon and was just about to put it in his mouth when he saw that the cousins were picking up whole dumplings from the stew with their fingers and stuffing them in their mouths. Then they licked their fingers, wiped their mouths on their yellow scarves, picked up their bowls and gobbled up the stew, without using with a spoon or anything else. They both made a noise like pigs feeding from a trough. Then both cousins wiped their mouths with the backs of their hands.

Gabby pretended he had not seen what they were doing as he put a spoonful of stew into his mouth. His cousins stared at him in amazement.

'Whatever is you a-doin' of, cousin,' asked Gideon, 'Why's you puttin' that little old piece of iron in your mouth? Don't it make this here fine stew taste of rust?'

'Certainly not,' snapped Gabby and carried on eating. Not that he enjoyed it, because his cousins were watching him with wide eyes as he ate.

He finished his stew and sat back to wait for pudding. Then he realised that the cousins were staring at him.

'Hey, cousin,' protested Grethel, 'It's shockin' bad manners to eat your grub all quiet like you did and even worse not to wipe your mouth with your hand afterwards.'

Mother, who was in the kitchen, heard Gabby shouting, 'No, it is *not*! Eating like pigs and using your hands instead of a napkin might be good manners where you come from. But not here in Tinseltown!'

'Well,' drawled Grethel, 'If that's how you folks eat, I would feel sick at every meal and I sure ain't stayin' here. C'mon, brother, let's git the bus back home, quick. Folks there eats their chow properly and don't have disgustin' manners like some I could mention. So long, cuz. So long, Aunt. Be seein ya!'

The cousins marched upstairs, packed their bags and walked out. And that was the last that Tinseltown ever heard of them.

The message is

Your ideas about table manners may not suit other people.

Share your thoughts with everyone ...

What do some of us use instead of knives, forks and spoons?

What *are* bad table manners?

Are table manners the same everywhere?

Think quietly about

Making sure that your own table manners do not upset other people.

Saying 'Thank you' for the buying and cooking of your food

The people who grow our food.

Songs to sing

One potato two potato	*Apusskidu* 31
Pears and apples	*Come & Praise* 135
Dip and fall back	*Mango Spice* 5
Oats and beans	*Music Box Song Book* 14
Ten fat sausages	*Okki-Tokki-Unga* 38
Sticky side down	*Sing it in the Morning* 59
Pepper song	*Sing it in the Morning* 62

Prayers

Page 218

23 It's my last sweet

Theme

Sharing.

Some children are more than generous, especially with close friends. Some, unfortunately, share to impress or to 'buy' friends.

We should try to persuade children to develop the quality of 'sharing' for the best possible reasons, or, putting it another way, being unselfish.

Let's talk

If you had a bag of sweets would you share them with your friends?

Do you share your toys with friends? Why?

Who would give their last sweet to a friend? Why?

Who would give their last sweet to someone who was crying, even if you didn't know the boy or girl? Why?

Time to listen

I told you a story about poor Giraffe, whose coat changed colour because she stayed in the sun too long. This is what happened afterwards.

The Yumyum Fruit and the Scorpion

Giraffe was so upset about spoiling her beautiful coat in the sun that she went about in a daze, not caring what happened. As she wandered, she blundered into a yumyum tree and a big, purple fruit fell off a high branch, landing on the soft earth. There it was spotted by Scorpion, a grumpy creature, with a tail that ended in a nasty-looking sting.

'Humf,' grunted Scorpion, 'This looks jolly tough and I don't like purple fruits, anyway, but I saw it first. So it's mine, even if I don't want it.' She clambered on to the top of the yumyum fruit and crouched there, her quivering tail sticking up in the air. As she stood, hissing and looking most unfriendly, along came Spotted Snake.

'Hello, Scorpion. That's a fine purple fruit you have there,' he said, cheerfully, 'How about a chunk?' But, before he could say any more, Scorpion lashed out with her vicious tail, just missing Spotted Snake's shiny nose, and hissed, 'Clear off. Leave my fruit alone. It's mine, all mine'. Spotted Snake changed his mind and glided away.

Then along came Bullfrog, who croaked, 'Hello, Scorpion, my old friend. My, what a fine fruit you have there. How about ...'

Old friend or not, Scorpion did her best to sting him, hissing as her tail whipped past Bullfrog's head, 'Clear off. Leave my fruit alone. I'm not sharing it with anyone.' Bullfrog opened his big mouth to say something, thought better of it and hopped away.

Scorpion was just as unkind to Iguana, Bat, and even Macaw, who is a kind of parrot and after a while everybody left her alone with the yumyum fruit.

She was just nodding off to sleep when the ground began to shake and the scorpion heard a sound that grew ever louder. *Tramp, tramp, tramp, tramp*. It was the Feared Giant Ant Army.

'Clear off!' hissed Scorpion, waving her tail furiously. 'I found this fruit and it is all mine. I'm not sharing it with anyone!' But Scorpion had never seen the Feared Giant Ant Army on the march. Not only did they take no notice of Scorpion's tail and sting but they marched right over her and ate every scrap of the yumyum fruit.

And, Giant Ants being what they are, they ate Scorpion while they were at it.

The message is

You are unlikely to be eaten if you do not share what you have, but sharing is a kind thing to do.

Share your thoughts with everyone

Will people think you are a much nicer person if you do share?

What are they likely to do if you share with them?

Should you share because someone says you have to?

Are there times when it is better *not* to share with others?

What do we call a person who has a lot of sweets/crisps/toys and will not share them with other children?

(*Look for 'dog in a manger' – perhaps follow up with the fable up on another occasion.*)

Think quietly about

Times when you have refused to share with others.

Promising yourself that you will share when it is right to do so.

Songs to sing

Both sides now	*Alleluya* 33
I'm going to paint	*Come & Praise* 83
The hungry man	*Every Colour* 32
Seeds of kindness	*Every Colour* 42
The ants go marching	*Okki-tokki-unga* 36
I belong to a family	*Sing it in the Morning* 3

Prayers

Page 218

24 Who will hold your hand?

Theme

Encouraging independence of adults. Many children who can operate quite sophisticated electronic equipment are unable to (or don't want to ...) perform basic tasks. Perhaps they need a nudge?

Let's talk

Who can operate a TV/video recorder/hifi/etc?

Who makes their own bed?

Tell us about some of the things you can do at home.

Time to listen

This is another story about Princess Splendid who thought she was *so* important ...

Castaway Princess

'Gloria! Bring me a chocolate!' said Her-Ever-So-Highness Princess Splendid. Her lady-in-waiting handed a chocolate to the Princess who looked at it and threw it back at her.

'You stupid creature!' screeched the Princess, 'This is toffee! You know I only like soft centres. Go and run my bath.' Gloria rushed off, almost colliding with His Jolly-High-Up Majesty King Posh outside the door.

'Good morning!' he chortled. 'My daughter being bossy again, what? Never mind, we are soon going to visit my cousin King Floss. So you can have a holiday.'

A week later, as the Royal Yacht was sailing to Candy Island, it ran into a terrible storm and sank. Princess Splendid was washed up on a white, sandy beach, where she fell asleep. She awoke to find a boy of about twelve years old staring at her.

'You're all wet,' said the boy, whose name was Robinson, as he walked away.

The Princess sat up and shrilled, 'Don't you speak to me like that, boy!

I am a Princess and you must do as I tell you. Come back here at once!' But the boy had disappeared.

The Princess wandered up the beach until she saw a hut built from branches and palm leaves. A delicious smell of food came from inside. Her tummy rumbled, telling her that she was hungry, and she went into the dark hut.

The boy, Robinson, who was inside, grinned at her and asked, 'Do you want some fish stew?'

Princess Splendid said 'Yes, please.'(She had learnt some manners from Wizard Stickler!) Robinson waved his fork at the stewpot that was on the fire and told her to get a dish and spoon and help herself.

'Certainly not,' said the Princess haughtily, '*You* must get it for me. I am much too royal to do things like that.'

Robinson chuckled, 'Not here you aren't. If you want anything done, you'll have to do it yourself.' And for the next six months, until they were rescued, the Princess had to do her share of finding food, fishing and cooking. She got quite good at it, too.

After she and Robinson were rescued, I expect you think that she became a different person when she got home again? Oh, dear me, no. She went straight back to her old ways and never ever did anything for herself again. Of course, if you knew Her-Ever-So-Highness Princess Splendid as well as I do, you wouldn't be surprised, either.

The message is

You should not expect grown-ups or other children to do everything for you.

Share your thoughts with everyone

Who would know what do if someone fell ill or had an accident and you were alone?

Songs to sing

Points of view	*Every Colour* 45
Do your best	*Every Colour* 48
Each day different	*Harlequin* 43
Can anyone tell me that?	*Tinderbox* 6
New things to do	*Tinderbox* 58

Prayers

Page 218

25 Playing your part

Theme

Everybody who is part of a family has a responsibility to the rest of the family, if they are able. This is true at home and at school.

Let's talk

*Tell us about jobs you are expected to do at home.

or

What sort of jobs should children be expected to do at home?

Time to listen

This is a story about three plump, pink little pigs called Pickle, Peppy and Poggy and it is a little different from the story about three pigs that you may have heard before.

Why Me?

Wilhelmina, a hungry lady wolf, fancied plump pigs for her supper. So she huffed and she puffed and easily blew down Pickle's house that was made of straw.

Next, the hungry lady wolf huffed and puffed and easily blew down Peppy's house that was made of wood.

Both little pigs ran squealing to Poggy's house that was made of bricks and scampered indoors just in time to escape Wilhelmina.

When the wolf arrived at Poggy's house, she huffed and puffed and puffed and huffed until she was panting for breath and her long, purple tongue was hanging out. But, no matter how hard she blew, Poggy's house would not fall down, because it had been built so strongly.

A week later, the three little pigs sat down to eat supper. Poggy wiped the last of the custard off his chinny-chin-chin, and said, 'Time for bed, little pigs. Pickle, did you lock and bolt the front door? We don't want that big bad wolf in here, do we?'

Pickle twitched his little, snub snout and grunted, 'Er, no. I didn't. I locked it last night. It's Peppy's turn tonight.'

Peppy squealed, 'Oo, you did no such thing. *I* locked it last night. And the night before. So there.'

Pickle snorted angrily, 'You never. You've only locked the door once since we came here.'

Then he turned to Poggy and said spitefully, 'Anyway, this is *your* house and if anyone should lock the door at night, it should be *you*. Not us.'

Peppy joined in, saying, 'Yes, why should we? Just because *you* say so. It isn't fair.'

Angry Poggy banged his trotter on the table, making all the dishes dance up and down. Then he opened his mouth to speak. Instead, his face went very pale and he stared at the doorway. His cousins' beady little eyes followed Poggy's stare.

'Good evening, boys,'said Wilhelmina Wolf, who was leaning against the door frame, her long, white teeth gleaming in the lamplight, 'How nice of you to leave the door unlocked so that I could visit you. You know, I do believe it is supper-time.'

The message is

It is no use leaving a job for someone else to do if you are supposed to do it yourself.

Share your thoughts with everyone

In which ways can we help in school and at home without actually doing any jobs.

Think quietly about

Whether we need to be grown-up to make ourselves useful.

Songs to sing

If you're happy	*Apusskidu* 1
I can climb	*Every Colour* 17
A house is a house for me	*Tinderbox* 13
Mama don't 'low	*Tinderbox* 21
Why does it have to be me?	*Tinderbox* 53

Prayers

Page 218

26 Birds in their little nests agree

Theme

The futility of quarrelling.

Let's talk

Do you ever quarrel with anyone?

Where? Why?

Who wins?

Time to listen

I hope you don't squabble like this at home.

Uncle Bruce and Ozzie Prezzies

Uncle Bruce had lived in Australia for many years, long before the twins Dinah and Dillon were born.

One day, he arrived to stay with the family for a few weeks and after lunch he told the children, 'I've got some great Ozzie goodies for you kiddies.' He gave Dinah a large toy kangaroo, and a large toy koala bear to Dillon. Neither twin thanked him, which seemed to surprise him a little, but he put on his hat and went out.

The door had only just closed on him when Dillon growled at his twin sister, 'I don't like this stupid bear thing. Boys don't have silly fluffy toys. Gimme yours,' and he snatched the toy kangaroo from Dinah.

She let out a loud screech and snatched it back again. Dillon pulled her hair, Dinah replied by kicking Dillon, then she grabbed the kangaroo. Dillon would not let go, there was a ripping sound and the kangaroo burst, scattering stuffing everywhere. The empty skin – which wasn't real, of course – fluttered down and lay, sadly, on the carpet.

'Now look what you've done, you horrible boy!' shrieked Dinah and she picked up Dillon's koala bear and jumped on it. Of course that burst too, so all they had left were two empty toy skins. The children then attacked one another with teeth and nails until Mum packed them off to bed without any supper.

When Uncle Bruce came back and was told that it had all happened as a result of one of their many quarrels, he was most annoyed. He decided that he would move on to visit an old friend who lived in Scotland and had no children. The twins were sorry because Uncle Bruce probably had a lot to tell them about Australia.

The only person who was pleased was Mum because Uncle Bruce had said at lunchtime that he might stay for another month and he had a huge appetite. Mind you, she was not at all pleased with the reason for his departure, and the twins were not allowed to go out for a week.

The message is

Nobody gains anything from quarrelling.

Share your thoughts with everyone

Does anyone enjoy quarrelling? Why?

Why do people quarrel?

What is the worst kind of quarrelling?

Think quietly about

Whether your last quarrel did anyone any good.

Songs to sing

Both sides now	*Alleluya* 33
You've got to move	*Come & Praise* 107
It's a great, great shame	*Every Colour* 44
Do your best	*Every Colour* 48
How do you feel today?	*Play School Song Book* 1
The angry song	*Tinderbox* 9

Prayers

Page 218

27 Friends are precious

Theme

The value of friendship.

Let's talk

Is it best to have one best friend or a lot of friends?

Who knows a grown-up who has had a best friend for a long time?

Time to listen

Long, long ago in Arabia, there were genies that lived in bottles. If you let one out of a bottle you could command him, or her, to bring you anything that you wanted.

Through Thick and Thin

Banazan was a young genie who had never left his bottle, and so his powers were fresh and great. One day, a poor man called Ahmed opened his bottle and out came a puff of smoke. This soon changed into a huge genie – Banazan!

'What is thy wish, Master?' he asked of Ahmed, 'Dost thou want gold or precious jewels or a great palace? Speak, for thy wish is my command.'

But Ahmed wanted none of these. All he asked was that Banazan should call him friend and that, in return, he would be a true friend to the genie. Banazan was amazed at such a simple request but said, 'It shall be so, Master.' Ahmed then told the genie that he was free to grant wishes to anyone he chose.

And so it was that many people found that Banazan the genie would give them anything they wanted and, as you would expect, they decided he was the finest fellow in the world, genie or not. Everyone told him that he was the best friend that they had ever had and the foolish genie believed them all.

But one day Haji, a trader in silk, asked Banazan for a herd of one thousand camels.

Of course, Banazan said, 'Thy wish is my command, O friend,' and he said the magic words which only genies can say. But, oh! disaster! He had used his powers so often in pleasing his new friends that no strength was left in his magic.

The genie vanished into his bottle and and sulked while Haji raved about his bad luck. Just then along came Ahmed and the miserable genie told him the sad tale.

Ahmed said, wisely, 'This may be for the best, Banazan. None of those greedy people were real friends. All they wanted was something for nothing. But all I want from you is your friendship.'

Banazan was a happy genie when he went to sleep and, although he found next morning that his happiness had given him back his powers, he never used then again for those people who had taken advantage of him.

As he told the High Genie when they next met, true friends are all one needs for happiness. Even a genie.

The message is

True friends will stick with you through bad times and good.

Share your thoughts with everyone

Have you ever been let down by anyone who had made a promise to you?(Avoid names)

Would you still think of that person as a friend? Why?

Think quietly about

Promising yourself that *you* will never let friends down if you can help it.

Songs to sing

A living song	*Come & Praise* 72
I can climb	*Every Colour* 17
We want to sing	*Sing a Silver Lining* 7
Friends	*Sing a Silver Lining* 15
I belong to a family	*Sing it in the Morning* 3
Thank you for my friends	*Tinderbox* 31
You and I	*Tinderbox* 55

Prayers

Page 218

28 And I should know

Theme

Holding a dogmatic opinion is not always wise.

Let's talk

Do you know people who always think they are right – even if they aren't?

What can we do about it?

Time to listen

Are grown-ups *always* right? Do you enjoy catching them out?

I am Never Wrong

'I think we turn left at this pub, Dad,' said Millie, from the back of the car, 'What a funny sign it has. Fancy calling a pub 'The Goose and Pudding'.

'Yes, Dad,' said my brother Martin, laughing, 'And, according to the map, the road past the pub meets the road to Lugston Magna. We go right at the crossroads there which is the road to Tollyton-on-Sea.

'Rubbish!' barked Mr Pogwaite. 'What do children know about it? I know which way to go. I often drove along here many years ago and I'm not likely to forget the way to Tollyton-on-Sea. I don't need *maps.* We turn *right* not left here, through Chickham and meet the Tollyton road at Lumpwide. You'll see.'

'Excuse me, dear,' said Mrs Pogwaite, 'But you did say you haven't been this way for some time, and perhaps the children are right this time.'

'I know how to find my way around England,' snapped the annoyed Mr Pogwaite, as he banged the steering wheel in temper, 'I *never* lose my way! You should know that!'

Mrs Pogwaite sighed and said, 'If you say so, dear,' she said.

Half an hour later Mr Pogwaite growled, 'Martin, have you got that map upside-down because all these stupid signposts point to somewhere called Tanglecap and none of them say Chickham nor Lumpwide?'

'Perhaps you've made a mistake, Dad,' suggested Millie.

Her father choked and bellowed, 'Mistake? Mistake? If I say it *is* the right road then it *is* the right road,' and he turned the car left on to a narrow lane. An hour later the car emerged on to a long straight road.

'Ah-hah!' crowed Mr Pogwaite, 'I told you I was right. This is the road. I recognise it! If I say I will find a way then I *will*. And I have.'

'Dad,' said Millie, trying not to laugh as she looked out of the window, 'Dad, isn't that the pub with the funny name again? The one we passed an hour ago?' Mr Pogwaite slammed on the on brakes so hard he nearly broke everyone's neck. The car screeched to a halt and he stared at the pub sign as if he could not believe his eyes.

The sign said, 'The Goose and Pudding.'

The message is

Some people can't help being know-alls.

Share your thoughts with everyone

Can we try to be kind to people who think they are always right?

Should we be rude to them or make a joke of it?

What if they don't think it is funny if they are wrong?

Think quietly about

Trying hard to be patient with people who think they are always right.

Songs to sing

I may speak	*Come & Praise* 100
Stick on a smile	*Every Colour* 43
Points of view	*Every Colour* 45
Magic penny	*Sing it in the Morning* 7
The angry song	*Tinderbox* 9
You'll sing a song	*Tinderbox* 30

Prayers

Page 218

29 Somebody has to come second

Theme

Winners and losers.

Let's talk

Which is more important – winning a race or taking part?

Is it wrong to enjoy winning?

Should we always try to win?

Would you make a fuss if you expected to win a competition and didn't?

Time to listen

The racers in this story had a nasty surprise!

Sabrina and a Disappointment

Every year in Slitherland, all the snails make their way to the Slimytown stadium to watch the exciting Shellolympics. Everyone enjoys the contests like the long skid, the tug-of-slime, the shell-bumping and the sliding races.

Of course, the snails don't run in their races – they slide along on their tummies because a snail has only one foot – which is its tummy!

Sabrina Swirl was sure she would win the exciting 5 metre slide once again. She had trained hard on Mr Gardener's patio and he was furious when he saw all the silver snail trails that Sabrina had left behind. Not that he could not do much about it except clean them up.

The Shellolympics are held in the Snail Stadium behind Mr Gardener's garage. A huge crowd of snails was there, all cheering for their own favourite, even a crowd of French snails shouting for their champion, Escargot, although nobody seemed to know how they had got there.

Everybody enjoyed all the events and then came the time for the important 5 metre slide. To everyone's surprise, the loudspeakers boomed out an announcement, 'Fellow snails, we have a late entry for this event!

Here, all the way from Africa is Giant Snail, Maxi Smootha!' The cheering stopped and every snail in the stadium gasped as they saw Maxi. He was as big as a frog, the biggest snail any one had ever seen!

The racers lined up, the starting gun banged and they were off! It is hardly surprising that Maxi crossed the finishing line before any of the other racers had slid just one metre.

Sabrina came second but, as she said when she had collected her medal, 'You can't win them all, so it never pays to boast about being a winner. Especially if you are not prepared for surprises.'

The message is

You can't expect to win every competition you enter.

Share your thoughts with everyone

Do you think the 5 metre slide was a fair race?

Why or why not?

Think quietly about

Not being *too* disappointed if you lose a race or don't win a prize in a competition.

Songs to sing

We are climbing	*Come & Praise* 49
You've got to move	*Come & Praise* 107
Caterpillars only crawl	*Harlequin* 26
Small is beautiful to be	*Play School Song Book* 22
Ready, steady, off we go	*Sing a Song of Celebration* 58
I can do most anything	*Sing a Song of Celebration* 59

Prayers

Page 218

30 Leave it tidy!

Theme:

Clearing up after oneself.

Children are probably no worse at clearing up after themselves than adults. If, however, they can be encouraged to ensure that work places and domestic areas are left clean and tidy after use, this can only be beneficial to all.

Let's talk

Who likes painting (art) lessons best of all?

What happens to the brushes and paints after you have finished?

Are there any other lessons that make a mess?

What happens when (any of those lessons) are over?

Time to listen

This story suggest that it doesn't pay to be careless.

The Trackers

The Chowkee braves, Light Foot and Clever Hand, had been very careless. Foolishly, they had chased a deer to the edge of the Nalamo village. The Nalamo were a bad-tempered tribe who did their best to shoot tresspassers with musket or bow-and-arrow.

There they had the bad luck to be spotted by Chief Sharp Owl's squaw, Bright Feather. She shouted so loudly that a party of grumpy Nalamo braves woke up and chased after the hunters, who had fled for their lives. Light Foot and Clever Hand rode hard until night fell, when they made camp in the Grizzly Woods and slept, exhausted.

In the morning, Light Foot was woken by Clever Hand, shaking him gently as he held out a leg of roast hare, speared on his knife.

'Come, eat,' said Heavy Hand, 'We must be on our way. The Nalamo trackers cannot be far behind us.' Light Foot took the leg, and ate the delicious meat off the bone, which he sucked clean and threw under a bush. Then the two braves rode on over the plain until they reached Clear

Water lake at sunset, where they slept for the night. They would reach safety at their home village in the morning.

The dawn air was cold when Light Foot woke with a start and looked up at the grinning faces of six war-painted Nalamo braves. Their leader, Frog Hopper, was pointing a nasty-looking spear at Light Foot's throat, while Buffalo Horn was pointing an even nastier-looking spear at Clever Hand's stomach.

'Get up, Chowkee fools,' hissed Frog Hopper, 'Very slowly.'

Light Foot looked desperately across at Clever Hand and wailed, 'How did they track us? We left no trail.' The Nalamo braves burst into mocking laughter. Frog Hopper held up his spear in one hand and, in the other – a small bone.

'Oh, no,' whispered Light Foot, 'It is the hare's leg-bone that I threw on the ground at our first camp.'

The leader sneered, 'So it is. You should have learned always to bury your rubbish. This is so because we Nalamos are the best trackers in the world. And now we shall teach you both a different lesson.'

What the lesson was, I cannot even guess but I cannot think that it was one that the Chowkee braves enjoyed.

The message is

There are times when failing to clear up after yourself could cause a great deal of trouble.

Share your thoughts with everyone

Are there times when you don't like eating at a table where someone has already been eating?

Do you always clear up after yourself?

Are there times when clearing-up is best left to other people?

Think quietly about

People who spend their lives cleaning up and cleaning up after others – binmen, road cleaners, school cleaners and so on.

People who clear up after accidents: doctors, nurses, ambulance workers, police, firefighters, all kinds of rescue people, demolition men and others.

Songs to sing

Keep the countryside tidy	*Every Colour* 14
Because you care	*Every Colour* 31
Across the hills	*Jolly Herring* 18
The tidy song	*Music Box Song Book* 27
Litterbin song	*Play School Songbook* 27
	Tinderbox 47
I would like to be	*Tinderbox* 45

Prayers

Page 218

*31 Wise heads on old shoulders

Theme

The much older generation.

Many children have special relationships with grandparents or other elderly relatives.

Let's talk

What do we mean by an 'old person'?

How old is old?

Who knows any old people?

Are they related to you or just someone you know?

Tell us about them.

Time to listen

Old people often know about things that younger people do not, and George found that out.

The Shoemakers

George makes and mends all the shoes of the people who live in Tubbywick, very quickly.

George uses all sorts of wonderful gadgets in his little shop for his shoe making and mending. All these clever machines work from a waterwheel that is driven by the stream that rushes under George's shop.

One day, as George was using a holeplonker that made laceholes in boots and shoes, his eighty-year-old father, Henry, came into the shop. He, too, had been a shoemaker and had taught George how to make and mend shoes without using machines – all he used were a hammer, a sharp knife and a needle and thread.

The old man watched George making laceholes with a machine, a strange smile on his wrinkled face.

'That is a clever machine, my son,' he said, thoughtfully, 'But what if the stream stops driving the waterwheel? Can you do those things without a machine?'

George became angry with his father and snapped, most rudely, 'The stream won't dry up. It hasn't done so in a hundred years! Anyway, what does an old fool like you know about modern machines. anyway? In fact, you're too old to understand about anything very much.'

Henry grinned as he left the shop, saying, 'We shall see, my son.' Then, strangely, the following week, the stream stopped flowing and the machines would not work any more! George did not know what to do.

He rushed to ask his father's advice. Henry told him to go back to the old ways of the shoemaker, even if it took longer than it did with the machines.

The stream began to flow again a few weeks later and, although George could use his machines once more, he had to admit that sometimes older people do know better than the young ones. Not only that, but young people can learn from old people, too.

Share your thoughts with everyone

What can children do to help old people?

What can children learn from old people?

Think quietly about

What it might be like to be old.

Why some young people often think old people are moaning, are stupid and are a nuisance.

Making up our minds to be kind to any old people that we know.

Songs to sing

Land of the old and grey	*Jolly Herring* 42
Helping Grandma Jones	*Music Box Song Book* 33
	Tinderbox 27
Grandma grunts	*Music Box Song Book* 36
Grandpa had a party	*Music Box Song Book* 46
When I'm sixty four	*Ta-ra-ra Boom-de-ay* 11
Slowly walks my grandad	*Tinderbox* 28

Prayers

Page 218

*32 Family friends

Theme

Caring for pets.

Most pets are well cared for, but some are not. Children often claim to have their own pet but leave it to another family member to do the feeding, and cleaning, and they should be encouraged to look after their own animals as far as possible.

Let's talk

Tell us what kind of animals can be kept as pets.

Tell us what kind of animals can *not* be kept as pets.

Tell us about your own pets at home.

(It could get out of hand ...!)

Time to listen

Goldfish can't really talk – this story pretends that they can.

How Would You Like to Be Me?

'Oi, Mister. Bubble bubble,' said a little hubbly bubbly voice that seemed to come from nowhere. Dale looked up from his book and looked round the room. Nobody there. He must have imagined the voice. He turned back to his book.

Then he heard the strange little voice again, 'Oi, Mister. Are you deaf, bubble, bubble?' Dale, a bit scared by now, looked round the room but all he could see was the fish tank in the corner which had Gwen the goldfish in it somewhere. He peered into the murky, green water. Dale could just make out the outline of the little fish that was blowing bubbles in a most peculiar way.

'At last! I thought you would never answer,' said the hubbly bubbly little voice which was coming from *inside the tank.*

Dale gasped, 'This is silly. Goldfish can't talk!'

Gwen pushed her little fishy nose against the dirty glass and said, 'Oh, yes, they can. Just because *you've* never heard one talking, it doesn't mean we *can't*, does it?'

'What do you want?' asked Dale, feeling rather stupid talking to a goldfish and hoping nobody was listening.

The goldfish said in her tiny, goldfishy voice, 'How about changing the water in my tank every week and feeding me every day instead of when someone thinks of it? It's called looking after me properly. People who don't look after pets shouldn't be allowed to keep them.' With that she swam away into a plastic castle.

Dale peered into the dirty water. As he did so, Gwen, the goldfish came out from the plastic castle, put her nose against the glass again and *winked* at him.

Which was very odd because … goldfish have no eyelids.

I wonder what happened after that?

The message is

Don't leave it to other people to look after your pets.

Share your thoughts with everyone

Tell me some ways in which we should look after our pets.

What should we do if a pet is ill?

Think quietly about

How much our pets depend on us.

Remembering that pets can't talk.

Songs to sing

Where, oh where, has my little dog gone?	*Apusskidu* 42
From the tiny ant	*Come & Praise* 79
Take care of a friend	*Every Colour* 35
A strange menagerie	*Play School Song Book* 19
You can't keep a horse in a lighthouse	*Ta-ra-ra-boom-de-ay* 23
You'll sing a song	*Tinderbox* 30
Any song from *Alphabet Zoo Book*	

Prayers

Page 218

GROWING UP

33 Speak kindly

Theme

An old saying but a true one – a soft answer turneth away wrath (Book of Proverbs 15:1).

Aggressive attitudes, in speech and action (such as 'road rage') seem to have become the norm for many people in modern society. We should, as educators, do all we can to encourage children to be more courteous to others, even under provocation. Admittedly, we are asking a lot of children who see such unsocial behaviour in daily life but, at least, we should try.

Let's talk

Someone new to the school sits in your dinner place (or other 'space' if 'dinner-place' does not fit your school).

Would you be annoyed?

What would you say and do?

You find someone you dislike taking your coat from the cloakroom.

The person says 'Sorry.'

What would you say and do?

Time to listen

In this story, the shopkeeper was rude to the wrong person …

The Stranger

The door-bell of the cheese shop tinkled and a smiling stranger, dressed in clothing patterned in green and yellow stripes, walked in. A fluffy feather stood up proudly from his pointed hat, while in his belt shone a bright golden flute.

'Greetings, good shopkeeper,' the stranger said cheerfully, 'Will you tell me how to find the Town Hall of this fine city?

Herman Gruber glared at him and growled, 'No, you fool in fancy clothes, I will not. This is a not a Tourist Office.'

The stranger's smile disappeared. He raised his sharp eyebrows and stroked his pointed beard.

'That is no kind way to speak to a stranger,' he said quietly.

Herman snapped, 'This is a cheese shop, not a parlour for practising manners. Did you not look at the sign over the door of my shop when you entered? Now push off before I help you on your way with my boot.' The stranger shook his head and took the golden flute from his belt.

'Indeed, I saw what kind of shop it was and thought I saw a friendly face within,' he said, a smile upon his dark face, 'But it matters not. No bones are broken. Now look upon my flute and listen to its song.'

Before Herman could answer, the stranger put the flute to his lips and a tune, as strange as the man himself and as golden as the flute, danced around the shop and floated away towards the River Weser that flowed just behind the shop.

Herman felt most peculiar. The eerie music stopped, and the cheese seller was unable to speak the unkind and unfriendly words that he had intended to say.

His lips felt thick and stiff and the words came out as, 'Why, of course, my dear sir, just go round the corner and you will see the Town Hall. Pray give his Worship the Mayor my best regards. Tell him that I shall be at the meeting tonight to discuss how we are to get rid of these dreadful rats that are eating our city bit by bit. And do have a pleasant day, won't you?'

Taking off his pointed hat and bowing, the stranger laughed and cried, cheerily, 'I thank you, good shopkeeper, you will not regret it.' With that, he left the shop, chuckling. And, ever since that day, Herman Gruber, cheese seller of the old German town of Hamelin, has never spoken unkindly to anyone again.

The message is

It is better to speak kindly than unkindly.

Share your thoughts with everyone

Have you ever spoken unkindly to other people?

Would you say you were rude?

Do you *always* speak unkindly to other people?

Or kindly?

Why?

Think quietly about

The times you have spoken unkindly to people in your home or school family or to strangers.

Whether you would do it again and why.

Songs to sing

Cross over the road	*Come & Praise* 70
A living song	*Come & Praise* 72
Seeds of kindness	*Every Colour* 42
Getting angry	*Every Colour* 46
How do you feel today?	*Play School Song Book* 1
Maja Pade – Let's all be happy	*Tinderbox* 57

Prayers

Page 219

34 Listen!

Theme

Paying attention when teaching is taking place.

As all teachers know children have a very short span of attention(once referred to as a low perseveration factor) and we can do little about it. What we can do, however, is to encourage children to listen closely when we want them to take something in.

Let's talk

Listen carefully. I shall say this only once.

Here are six words: green yellow dirty red blue purple.

Which of those words was *not* a colour?

(The response is unlikely to be 100%! – now read them again.)

Hands up who got it wrong?

Who can tell me why some of us got it wrong? (No reason why you should not prompt – 'They were not listening *properly*')

Time to listen

I hope you pay more attention to this story than Duggie Duckling might have done.

The Flying School

'Look, Mum, look, I'm flying!' quacked Duggie Duckling to his mother. who was swimming gently on the cold water of the lake.

After flapping his little wings furiously, he had made several hops so that, just for a few seconds, he had been running over the surface of the water until he splashed back in again.

Dora Duck had nodded her yellow beak and quacked, 'Yes, dear, very good. But I don't think you are *really* flying.' She waved a wing towards Gussie Goose who was just gliding towards the trees – 'Now *that* is flying. And, next week, you will be going to Flying School to learn how to fly – properly.'

'Huh,' grumbled Duggie to himself, 'I reckon I *was* flying and I don't need to go to Flying School.' But the following Monday, he had to go because his Dad said so.

'Right!' quacked Sergeant Delbert, Chief Flying Teacher. 'Let me see you swim as fast as you can and then how hard you can flap your little wings.'

Ten little ducklings swam as fast as they could, flapped their little wings as hard as they could and stretched their beaks up towards the sky.

As they swam and flapped and stretched and swam, the Sergeant quacked loudly at them, 'Faster, faster, stretch your necks upwards and swim faster!'

Then, to their surprise, nine of the ducklings found they were above the water and a little way in the air, then they splashed down again.

All except Duggie. Instead of swimming and stretching he was bobbing about on the water, dreaming about swooping and diving because he could fly already. Or so he thought.

Of course, we all know that he couldn't fly because he had not listened to anything the Sergeant had said. After three lessons, the other ducklings were really flying, with their little wings flapping busily away. But Duggie was still dreaming away, fooling himself that he could fly. By the time he realised what had happened, it was too late. Sergeant Delbert could be bothered to teach him. His dad had a try but he gave up, too.

And if you visit the lake today, you may see a very sad, grown-up duck watching the other ducks, big and small, soaring into the sky and swooping over the water as he sits on the water. You may think, 'Oh, poor duck. He's hurt his wing and can't fly.'

Don't feel sorry. That duck is Duggie.

The message is

You will never learn if you don't listen properly.

Share your thoughts with everyone

What should Duggie have done?

Think quietly about

Whether you spend time dreaming when you should be listening.

Making an effort to listen to people who know better than you do.

Songs to sing

I listen and I listen	*Come & Praise* 60
Do your best	*Every Colour* 48
Can you hear?	*Harlequin* 33
Six little ducks	*Okki-tokki-unga* 41
Sound song	*Tinderbox* 39
Try again	*Tinderbox* 56

Prayers

Page 219

35 Please let me finish

Theme

Interrupting when other people are speaking.

Let's talk

Teacher: Select a child to read a passage from a story and keep interrupting every now and again. Don't keep it up too long or the poor subject might become extremely stressed! Stop your pretence at the slightest sign …

What was I doing to (name of child)?

Was I being bad-mannered?

Do some children interrupt when another person is talking?

Is *that* bad manners?

Time to listen

Perhaps you can understand that nothing is more irritating than a person who interrupts when someone else is speaking.

Filbert and a Meeting

'Now,' said Chief Fieldmouse Frederick, 'Huge red monsters have been seen coming in ...

Young Filbert jumped up and down. 'Yes, yes, I saw them and they are *huge*!' he squeaked. Frederick sighed. Filbert was at it again.

'I was about to say something most important,' said the Chief. 'Now we do not know exactly what these red monsters ...'

'Oh, they make a *terrible* noise and kick up *dreadful* clouds of dust', chattered Filbert, 'My cousin Festus has seen them before.'

Frederick groaned. Filbert really was being a nuisance.

'I'm sure she has, but ... ' said the Chief of the Field Mice.

'My cousin is a *he*, Sir,' said Filbert, chipping in brightly, 'Not a *she*.'

Mopping his whiskers, Chief Frederick said, patiently, 'All right, *he*, I'm sorry. Now can we ...'

Filbert waved his paws about and squeaked, 'Oh, Sir, Chief Fieldmouse, Sir, please do not say you're sorry. It is a mistake that any mouse can make but I accept your apology, Sir, which is ...'

'Oh, do shut up, Filbert, you rude little mouse,' snapped Freda Fieldmouse, 'And stop interrupting the Chief Fieldmouse. Can't you understand that he has something important to say?'

Filbert stood up, sending the corn seats in all directions, his ears and whiskers quivering as he asked everybody, 'What I did do wrong, what did I do wrong?' All I said was ...' The Chief must have heard what Filbert said because he pointed at him and began to say something. Then he looked over Filbert's head and his tail stood straight up, quivering.

And, instead of telling Filbert off for interrupting, all he could say was, 'Run!' The little field mice scattered in all directions as the huge red combine harvester crushed the cornstook where they had been holding their meeting.

The message is

Sometimes interruptions can be more than just a nuisance.

Share your thoughts with everyone

Is interrupting only rude when children interrupt adults?

Think of some times when adults interrupt children.

Think of some times when grown-ups interrupt grown-ups.

Think quietly about

Whether *you* often interrupt other people.

Promising yourself that you will try hard not to interrupt other people, children or grown-ups.

Songs to sing

Turn, turn, turn	*Alleluya* 32
Points of view	*Every Colour* 45
Reach out	*Sing it in the Morning* 22
Side by side	*Ta-ra-ra-boom-de-ay* 36
You and I	*Tinderbox* 55
One, two, three	*Tinderbox* 65

Prayers

Page 219

36 I didn't like to ask

Theme

Did you really understand?

Children often give the appearance of understanding an idea or instructions when they have not really done so.

They usually do this because they do not wish to appear less bright than their peers or because they are too shy to ask. This is not the same as 'Listening but not hearing'(Assembly 34).

Let's talk

Who can understand this sentence? Dinosaurs are extinct.

Who would like me to explain what 'extinct' means?

It means that there are no dinosaurs left on earth; they have all died.

Who understands the sentence now?

If you cannot understand something you should ask it to be explained to you.

Time to listen

The two little boy hedgehogs learned a lot from their first attempt at camping.

Carry on Camping!

Hector and Hannibal had only been members of the Spikyton troop of Hedgehog Rangers for a month. Now they were unloading their camping gear in Farmer Nubb's Big Meadow. What fun it would be sleeping in a tent!

'Right, you two new Rangers,' called Troop-leader Higgysnip, 'Come here while I show you how to put up your tent.' She hammered poles into the ground, pulled ropes, and flapped sheets of canvas about, then stood back and beamed with pride at the neat little tent that she had just put up.

'Right. Now you know how to put up a tent,' she chirped cheerfully, 'Go and put up your own.'

But she had done it all too quickly for Hector and Hannibal to follow what she had done. The pair were too shy to ask the Troop Leader to explain it again and they weren't going to let the rest of the Troop think that they were stupid, were they? So they struggled away for ages until they had managed to put up something that looked like a tent.

Sadly, Mrs Higgysnip went to bed early with a headache. This meant she did not inspect what they had done.

Then, during the night, there was a huge rainstorm and the little hedgehogs woke up to find that the wet tent had collapsed on top of them and they were floating in their wet sleeping bags on a mini-pond.

Mrs Higgysnip blamed them for not saying that they hadn't followed her tent-putting-up lesson. Then she phoned Hector's dad to come and take them home to dry out.

He was not pleased with the little Rangers but he was really cross with the Troop Leader. He told her that she should have made sure that the boys knew what to do and it was just as much her fault as theirs. What do you think?

The message is

Don't be afraid to ask teacher if you don't understand something – after you have tried hard.

Share your thoughts with everyone

Should you *always* ask teacher to explain everything more than once?

Why not?

Should you get impatient with children who ask teacher to explain something again?

Think quietly about

Thinking first and trying hard before you ask for extra help.

Songs to sing

Holly the Hedgehog	*Alphabet Zoo Book* 24
You've got to move	*Come & Praise* 107
Do your best	*Every Colour* 48
Each day different	*Harlequin* 43
When I was a hedgehog	*Music Box Song Book* 68
New things to do	*Tinderbox* 58

Prayers

Page 219

37 Why are we waiting?

Theme

Patience!

Although we encourage (and the last Assembly positively suggests) children to ask for assistance, children new to school, and even those who have attended pre-school, often demand the *immediate* attention of teachers or anyone else involved.

They need a little persuasion to realise that, sometimes, they will just have to wait until the grown-up can give them the attention they seek.

Let's talk

If you need to show teacher the picture you have painted, and she(he) is busy, what should you do?

If she has to see three other children before you, what should you do?

If you need to go to the toilet in a great hurry, what should you do?

Time to listen

It's not easy being a baby dinosaur!

Two Dinosaurs and a Hole

Long ago, before there were any people, dinosaurs roamed the hot and dangerous earth and (so far as we know) all of them laid eggs, just as birds and crocodiles and turtles do today. One of the most fierce dinosaurs, which may have been an Allosaurus, made a hole in the hot sand of a scorching desert.

Then she laid two big eggs, covered them over with sand and left them to look after themselves. Weeks later, the eggs cracked open and the tiny dinosaurs struggled out into the hot sand at the bottom of the hole. There the babies lay, very tired after their efforts.

Boy dinosaur asked, 'What do we do now?'

Girl dinosaur said uncertainly, 'Get out of this hole when it gets dark and find somewhere safe to live, I suppose.'

Boy yawned and grumbled, 'I'm awfully hungry.'

Girl waved a claw at him and said, 'There are a lot of older dinosaurs out there, with much sharper teeth and claws than we have. They would enjoy a little snack'.

'Of what? asked Boy, who was not too bright.

Girl dinosaur groaned. 'Of baby dinosaur, stupid,' she snapped, showing her many teeth.' Boy stood up on his wobbly back legs, until his sister dragged him down again.

'Get down, stupid, ' she hissed, 'Just be patient until it's dark.'

Boy snarled, 'I can't wait until then. How am I going to grow into a strong dinosaur if I don't eat?' He scrambled out of the hole and on to the sizzling hot rock at the edge of the hole.

Girl dinosaur waved a claw after him and wailed, 'Come back, come back. You'll get ...'

Just then, a huge, black, winged shadow drifted across the hole. Girl heard a faint squealing and then ... there was silence.

The message is

There are times when it pays to be patient.

Share your thoughts with everyone

What do you think happened to Boy Dinosaur?

Why did it happen?

Tell us about some times when you should be patient.

Tell us about some times when you have *had* to be patient.

Tell us about some times when you have not been patient.

Did you do the right thing?

Think quietly about:

People who are ill and have to be patient.

Starving people who have to wait for food.

Sick people who have to wait for a doctor to help them.

Songs to sing

Take the time to cogitate	*Every Colour* 47
To ev'rything turn	*Come & Praise* 113
Time is a thing	*Come & Praise* 104
The prehistoric animal brigade	*Okki-tokki-unga* 8
Taking my time	*Songs for Every Day 61*
Mysteries	*Tinderbox 40*

Prayers

Page 219

*38 Feeling poorly?

Theme

Going to school when unwell.

Although many children will gladly stay at home if they feel unwell, there are two other categories of sufferers. The first is children who are pressed to go to school by parents or guardians because the adults have to go to work. Inevitably teachers have to pick up the pieces (hopefully that is all they have to pick up). Sadly, there is little that schools can do about this problem.

The second comprises children who are real little heroes. In other words, they insist on attending school even though they should not be there. Perhaps we *can* do something about them?

Time to listen

Glenn should have listened to his mother.

Spots and the School Play

'Glenn,' said Mrs Dissle anxiously 'Are you sure you are well enough to go to school? I don't like the look of those spots on your tummy.'

'Mum, I must,' Glenn squealed, 'Nobody else can be King George in our play, because I'm the only one who's learnt the words. And he started to recite, 'Here am I, King George the knight, come from foreign lands to fight, bring on the … '

'Yes, yes, yes,' groaned his mum, 'I think I've heard it before.' Glenn had been practising for weeks and his family were sick of the Mummers' play that his class were performing on St George's Day.

Glenn didn't want any breakfast, he felt all hot and sweaty when he went into Assembly and even worse in Literacy Hour.

Then at playtime he felt sick and he rushed out to the toilets and *was sick.* When he came back Miss Brook looked at him and saw that his face was covered in big red blotches.

'I'm going to ring your mum,' she said crossly, 'Were you feeling poorly before you came to school?' Glenn had to admit that he was but it was no good ringing his mum because she had gone shopping in Farnchester and would not be back until three o'clock and his dad was driving his lorry in Germany so it was no use expecting him to take him home was it?

Miss Brook told him not to be cheeky but said she would make allowances because he did not feel well. He would just have to spend the rest of the day in the cloakroom with the 'Not-very-well' bucket as it was called and she just hoped it wasn't catching.

But it was and the following day everybody in the school, including the teachers and the cook and the caretaker was covered in red blotches or spots or both and they had to shut the school for three days.

The doctor never found it what it was and the mysterious illness never returned, but Glenn got a long telling-off from Mrs Price, the Headteacher, for coming to school when he was poorly.

And she said that, as a punishment, he could not be King George in the play and Glenn would have to be the dragon's back legs instead.

That might help him to think of other people in future. Still, he was quite popular with the children because everyone had three days extra holiday.

The message is

If you feel really poorly, stay at home.

Share your thoughts with everyone

Why should you stay at home if you are unwell?

Who should look after you if you are ill in school?

Should you stay at home if you are not really unwell?

Think quietly about

Whether there have been times when you should have stayed at home.

How much trouble you can cause if you are ill in school.

Songs to sing

On a work day I work	*Every Colour* 24
Miss Polly	*Okki-tokki-unga* 17
Do your ears hang low?	*Okki-tokki-unga* 25
You can do it	*Sing a Silver Lining* 9
Monday morning	*Songs for Every Day* 6
I've got a body	*Tinderbox* 5

Prayers

Page 219

39 Easy to lose

Theme

Looking after your own property.

Let's talk

Who has lost anything in the past week/month?

What did you lose?

Was it your own fault?

Time to listen

When you say you have lost something, do you really mean you have *mislaid* it? In other words, you could probably find it if you tried hard enough – like Fluffpot.

A Tale of a Tail

Fluffpot came rushing in from the rain and ran, squealing, her fur wet and her ears and whiskers as droopy as a dead dandelion. 'Oh, Momma, what shall I do?' she howled.

Mrs Topwhiskas put down her magazine and said kindly, 'Now stop making that noise and come and tell me what's wrong.'

'I can't! My life is ruined! Oh, what shall I do?' Fluffpot squealed as she rushed out of the living-room and into her bedroom.

A little later, Mother went to find out what her kitten was up to. Peeping into the bedroom, she saw that Fluffpot was standing on her head and trying to see her rear end in a long mirror on the cupboard.

As Mrs Topwhiskas went into the room, Fluffpot lost her balance and crashed to the floor.

'Whatever are you doing?' asked her mother. Fluffpot sat up, her ears all floppy and sad.

'I don't know where my lovely, fluffy, white bobtail has gone,' she wailed, 'Everybody will laugh at me. I mean, whoever heard of a girl bunny without a bobtail? I shall have to stay indoors until I am a very old rabbit and ...' Mrs Topwhiskas began to laugh.

'There, I told you. Even my own mother is laughing at me,' whimpered Fluffpot.

'No, no, Fluffy,' chuckled Mrs Topwhiskas, 'I'm not laughing at you. Go and have a shower and give yourself a good rub all over. Especially your rear end.' Five minutes later Fluffpot danced into the living-room and flung her paws round her mother.

As she danced she squeaked happily, 'My lovely white bobtail is back, all fluffy and puffy.'

Mrs Topwhiskas smiled knowingly, and said, 'Of course it is,' she said, 'The rain made it stick to your fur. It wasn't lost at all, you silly bunny-kitten. Now, next time you think you have lost something, stop, think and look for it properly.' Fluffpot promised her Mum that she would. Just like you would, I'm sure. If you had a furry bobtail.

The message is

Always be certain that something is really lost before you start to panic. Remember – it is probably where you left it.

Share your thoughts with everyone

Is it easier to lose something than it is to find it?

If you do lose something, do you blame somebody else?

What should you do if you find out why you 'lost' it through your own fault and you have blamed someone else?

Think quietly about

The trouble caused when something is lost through carelessness.

The trouble caused when something precious is brought to school and lost in school.

Songs to sing

Do your best	*Every Colour* 48
The Losing Things song	*Songs for Every Day* 42
Give to us eyes	*Someone's Singing, Lord* 18
Hands to work and feet to run	*Someone's Singing, Lord* 21
Try again	*Tinderbox* 56

Prayers

Page 219

40 You'll be sorry!

Theme

Leave your treasures at home.

Bringing precious and expensive objects is probably more common among children from Year 3 onwards. Nevertheless, it is prudent to suggest, very early in the school career, that such belongings are best left at home whether valuable or not.

Let's talk

Who would like to tell us about the most important thing they own? (You may have to limit responses!)

Why is it so important?

(If the object is portable) Would you bring it to school for any reason?

Time to listen

The African chief in this story was sorry that he took his most precious possession with him when he went on a long journey.

The Chief and his Great Chair

Chief Imotu always sat in his Great Chair at meetings of the Inyati tribe's elders and chief warriors. He was very proud of this old chair, which was made from the finest woods and was cared for lovingly.

One day Imotu had to attend a meeting in the Royal Palace at Ymala. He disliked such meetings because the rich chiefs showed off some of the fine things they owned. As Imotu was poor, he had nothing to show and the other chiefs looked down their noses at him.

So, for this meeting he decided to show off his Great Chair because, as far as he knew, nobody had a chair quite like it. That would show them.

Eight of his strongest warriors set off, carrying the Great Chair upon their broad shoulders. All went well until they reached the Black Swamp. The Chief thought he knew the way through the swamp but he realised that he did not when, without warning, the warriors and the chair disappeared into the thick, black, smelly mud. They managed to scramble out, but it was hours before they rescued the chair, which by now was black and crusty and stank.

In the four days the journey took, the chair fell into a deep hole and was dropped twice as the party was chased, first by an angry warthog and then by a swarm of ferocious hornets. Then everybody – and the chair – plummeted off a rope bridge into the river and, as the warriors swam for their lives, a family of crocodiles sharpened their teeth on the chair. Two of the bravest warrriors had to retrieve the chair when the crocodiles were asleep.

By the time the travellers reached Ymala, it did not look much like a chair at all. One chief asked Imotu why had he had brought his own firewood with him and another wanted to know if he was now so poor that he had become a chair-mender.

Imotu was most upset, but he felt better when Queen Folati gave him a bag of gold to have it repaired, because she felt sorry for him. Even so, he had to pay out the two bags of gold and three cows besides for the chair to be repaired because it was so badly damaged.

You can be quite sure that Imotu never took anything precious with him on a journey – ever again.

The message is

Precious things are safer at home.

Share your thoughts with everyone

How would you feel if you took your best toy to school and someone broke it?

Whose fault would it be?

Is it a good idea to take special things to school?

Are there any times when it *is* a good idea to take special things to school?

Think quietly about

The trouble that can be caused when special things get damaged in school.

How you would feel if you broke something belonging to somebody else.

Songs to sing

Use your eyes	*Every Colour* 11
Each day different	*Harlequin* 43
Join in the game	*Okki-tokki-unga* 2
Growing	*Play School Song Book* 5
Can anyone tell me that?	*Tinderbox* 6
Thank you for my friends	*Tinderbox* 31

Prayers

Page 219

41 Are you ready?

Theme

Being ready for an event (even as minor as going to school or going home).

Children should be encouraged to prepare for an impending activity without being chivvied or assisted, unless absolutely necessary.

Let's talk

Tell me about some of things that need to be done before you leave home for school in the morning (dinner money, packed lunch, PE gear, reading books etc.)

What about home-time in school?

Time to listen

What a foolish grasshopper!

Gus and the Days of Autumn

As Gus Grasshopper wandered dreamily along the path in the woods, he bumped into Arabella Ant.

'Isn't it a lovely autumn day?' he said, yawning. 'I do love autumn, don't you?'

The little black ant replied, 'I do, Gus, I do, but I hate to think that winter will soon be here.'

Gus chuckled, 'You don't want to worry about winter on a day like this. Enjoy the sunshine and the winter will look after itself.'

'You'll be sorry, Gus,' said Arabella, anxiously, 'I have collected all the wood that I shall need to keep my little underground nest warm through the cold winter.'

Gus snorted, 'Ha! I shall be ready, never fear. But I'm not going to waste this lovely sunshine collecting wood. Plenty of time for that later.' With that, he went on his merry way through the warm days of autumn, not caring about anything.

Until, one morning, he woke up to hear the wind howling round the old rusty kettle which was his home. It was very cold and Gus found that he was shivering. He lifted the lid and peeped out. What he saw turned him from grasshopper green to snowy white!

Deep snow had fallen in the night. Autumn was over and winter had come very suddenly. Gus rushed to his woodshed. It was empty. The frightened grasshopper decided he must go into the woods to collect logs for his fire. He was too cold to hop, so he had to crawl. But grasshoppers are not built for crawling, especially through deep snow.

So far as I know, nobody ever saw him again, which is very sad. If only he had listened to his friends and been ready for winter!

The message is

It is wise to be ready for things that you know are going to happen.

Share your thoughts with everyone

Tell us some ways in which we can be ready for dinner.

Tell us some ways in which we can be ready to go on holiday.

Think quietly about

How you can help yourself to get ready to come to school.

Songs to sing

You've got to move	*Come & Praise* 107
Do your best	*Every Colour* 48
The North wind	*Music Box Song Book* 95
Weather song	*Music Box Song Book* 97
A time for everything	*Songs for Every Day* 25
Look for the silver lining	*Sing a Silver Lining* 5

Prayers

Page 219

42 Tomorrow, tomorrow

Theme

Two old sayings:

Don't put off until tomorrow what you can do today

and

Procrastination is the thief of time.

Let's talk

Who has ever started a job and put off finishing it until the next day – or even longer?

Did you finish the job?

Tell us about jobs that cannot be left until the next day (eg surgery, mending bridges, important machinery).

Time to listen

In this story Alfric leaves things a bit late.

Alfric and the Dragon

'Alfric!' Baron Bluster yelled from the other side of the castle moat, 'Bring me my sword at once! There's a very large, fire-breathing dragon out here and it wants a fight. I can't think why because I haven't done anything to annoy it.'

Alfric rushed to the window and saw the Baron glaring at a big, bright green dragon, which had orange smoke trickling from its nostrils. It was making little rumbling noises and, every now and then, little flames flickered through the smoke in the direction of the Baron.

He grabbed Bluster's sword from the corner of his room, rushed down the stairs, across the drawbridge and handed the sword to the Baron, who looked at it in disgust.

'You didn't get this sword sharpened, you stupid squire, did you?' he bellowed, 'I mean, look at it! Great chunks out of the blade and it is rusty! I can't possibly fight a dragon with this!'

Then the dragon saw the sword. It stopped rumbling and breathing smoke and flame and began to laugh. It laughed so much that it rolled on the ground, kicking its scaly legs and mopping its yellow eyes with a dragon hankie. Then it shook itself, stopped laughing, sat up and spoke, stopping to utter little sobs of laughter now and again.

'Oh, my dear Baron, you weren't really going to fight me with that rusty old ... ho ho ho ... sword, were you? I mean, you couldn't cut cheese with it, let alone a tough old fellow like me. It's quite put me off the idea of fighting you. I bet your squire put off getting it sharpened. As he's spoilt my day and made you look a fool, I think we should teach him a lesson, don't you?'

Baron Bluster nodded. And, if you had been watching, you would have seen Alfric jumping into the moat and yelling because his trousers were on fire, and wishing he had not put off a job that needed to be done.

As for the Baron and the dragon, they both went into the castle and had toast for tea. I wonder how they made the toast?

The message is

If you have to do something you might as well do it sooner rather than later.

Share your thoughts with everyone

Tell me about some more jobs that should never be put off until tomorrow or even longer.

Think quietly about

Those times when *you* put off doing a job and you should not have done so.

Whether it caused trouble for other people as well as yourself.

Songs to sing

Maggon, the bad-tempered dragon	*Appuskidu* 55
Do your best	*Every Colour* 48
I jump out of bed in the morning	*Okki-tonga-unga* 47
Song for a bragging dragon	*Silly Aunt Sally* 52
Can anyone tell me that?	*Tinderbox* 6
Puff, the magic dragon	*Tinderbox* 50

Prayers

Page 219

43 Fair Shares

Theme

Greediness.

Let's talk

If you have to share a pizza or a cake with someone, do you expect to have the biggest piece?

If you are at a party, would you eat the last piece of cake even if you had already eaten three pieces?

If you are eating a meal, should you go on eating until you can eat no more?

Time to listen

Bobkin certainly learnt a lesson in this Brockle story.

The Birthday Cake

Bobkin is a Brockle (you know, one of those very small persons not much bigger than your big toe). One day, as Bobkin watched his Mum mixing his birthday cake, the telephone rang and she went to answer it.

Looking at the mixture in the bowl, Bobkin muttered, 'Huh, this looks a bit boring. I'll make it a bit more exciting.' He took a handful of what looked like chocolate chips out of a big jar on the table and poured them into the cake mixture, stirring them in as fast as he could.

'What are you doing?' asked Mrs Bumble, coming back into the kitchen. 'Have you been eating my cake mixture?' But Bobkin had gone and Mrs Bumble did not bother to look at the cake mixture again.

The next day, the party guests arrived and sat down to enjoy the delicious things to eat that Mrs Bumble had prepared. Bobkin piled food on to his plate and gobbled it up, then he had a second helping of everything, then a third .... By the time he had finished that, there did not seem to be much left for anyone else.

His mother looked very annoyed but she said, 'I think we will have Bobkin's birthday cake now.' She cut the cake but, before everyone had finished singing 'Happy Birthday', Bobkin had blown out the candles and grabbed most of the cake, put it on his plate and, straight away, crammed it in his mouth.

Then his bulging cheeks went a most peculiar colour and the greedy little Brockle ran out of the room, making strange choking noises.

Instead of putting what he thought were chocolate chips into the cake mixture before it was cooked, Bobkin had put in peppercorns and mustard seeds!

She told him 'You should have taken a fair share and not been so greedy. Serves you right.' Bobkin was ill for three days but I'm still not sure if he learned his lesson.

The message is

Greedy people usually pay for their habits.

Share your thoughts with everyone

Are people only greedy about food?

What else might they want more than their fair share of?

Think quietly about

The times when you may have been greedy and wished you hadn't.

Songs to sing

Turn, turn, turn	*Alleluya* 32
A living song	*Come & Praise* 72
The hungry man	*Every Colour* 32
Friends	*Sing a Silver Lining* 15
I belong to a family	*Sing it in the Morning* 3
When a dinosaur's feeling hungry	*Tinderbox* 12

Prayers

Page 219

44 I'm no good at anything

Theme

Lack of self esteem.

Let's talk

Should children be expected to do the same things as grown-ups?

Tell me some things that children can do just as well as grown-ups.

Tell me some things children *cannot* do as well as grown-ups.

Does that make them unable to do their own thing?

Time to listen

This story is about Robin Hood's Merry Men – or a not-so-merry boy, anyway.

Harold Blows his Horn

'What's the matter, lad?' cried Friar Tuck. He smiled down at Harold, who was staring into the camp fire and looking very unhappy.

'I can't do anything, Father,' said Harold miserably, 'I'm twelve years old, Robin Hood's youngest Outlaw and all I can do is to blow a hunting-horn.'

'What about the Sherwood Forest Feast tomorrow?' said the Friar. 'I'm sure you will do well at some of the children's contests like the archery, wrestling, racing and tree-climbing.'

'I expect I will make a fool of myself, as usual,' whined Harold.

'Oh, I am sure you will do well,' laughed the plump monk, 'And you never know when blowing a hunting-horn could come in useful.' Harold grunted and went to bed.

But he did not do well. His arrows all missed the target, he fell out of a tree when he was climbing and he came last in his race round the Ring of Ten Oak Trees. Worst of all, in the wrestling he was thrown to the ground in just one minute by Eleanor, daughter of John the Fletcher.

Harold was so upset that he ran off into the bushes so that nobody would see him crying with shame. But, as the boy sat there, he heard the tramp of marching feet and the thud of horses' hooves. Harold peeped out and saw, to his horror, dozens of the Sheriff of Nottingham's soldiers, heading straight for the camp and the Outlaws.

He did not hesitate but climbed quickly up a tree and blew a warning on his hunting-horn. Quick as a flash the outlaws melted into the forest. Soldiers fired arrows at Harold but he was down the tree and away into the forest before anybody could chase him.

The next day, he was hailed as a hero by Robin Hood and the whole band of Outlaws. And Harold never felt useless again.

The message is

Everybody can be good at something.

Share your thoughts with everyone

I do not think you will be boasting if you can tell me about:

Something you can do well.

Something you think you can do better than anyone else in your class/group.

Why do you say you can do this?

Think quietly about

Whether you think you are one of those who cannot do anything.

Would you think again?

Songs to sing

I can climb	*Every Colour* 17
Do your best	*Every Colour* 48
Caterpillars only crawl	*Harlequin* 26
Try again	*Music Box Song Book* 26
You can do it	*Sing a Silver Lining* 9
New things to do	*Tinderbox* 58

Prayers

Page 219

45 It's surprising

Theme

You can do many things if you make up your mind to do them.

Let's talk

* *Note: This assembly may need a careful approach if you have children with special physical needs in your school.*

Who thinks they are good at painting pictures?

Who thinks they are good at writing?

Tell me some other things for which you need your hands.

Would you be as good at them if you had *no* hands?

Time to listen

What do we call a 'made-up story'? (fiction)

This is not fiction and it is not really a story – Billy Collins was a real person.

You've Never Heard of Him But ...

I am going to tell you about a boy who had a terrible accident, about the time when your great-grandparents were children.

The boy's name was Billy Collins and the accident happened when he was only 14 years of age. He worked in a factory where bricks were made. Billy did not mind the job he was doing although it was dirty and he earned very little money for what he did.

But, one day, something dreadful happened to Billy – he was dragged into one of the machines at the factory and, when he woke up, the poor little boy had no arms.

In hospital, nurses fed him with a spoon but Billy soon made up his mind that he was going to feed himself. I don't know how he did it, but he did, before he left hospital, after just five weeks.

As soon as he could, the boy went back to work at the brick factory. He could not work where the bricks were made, so he was given a job in the office. Here, Billy taught himself to write with a pencil *in his mouth* and, after some years, he was made chief of the office.

As he grew up, he made up his mind that he would do almost everything that could be done by a person who had both arms. Billy taught himself to draw and paint and how to play the piano.

He got married and had children and grandchildren and led a happy life like anyone else. This brave man was never miserable and helped many people who had lost arms or legs in accidents.

So, next time you have to have a plaster on a cut finger, or you have toothache, just think – it's not as bad as you think.

The message is

* *Rephrase this if you have a child who has problems with limbs*

If Billy Collins could do all these things with no arms what can you do *with* them?

Share your thoughts with everyone

Did you find this true story hard to believe?

* How would you feel if you had no arms or you could not use the ones you do have?

Would you feel sorry for yourself?

Think quietly about

Making up your mind never to be miserable if you have something that stops you from playing games.

Songs to sing

Travel on	*Come & Praise* 42
Guess how I fee	*Come & Praise* 89
Song of life	*Every Colour* 22
On a wonderful day like today	*Sing a Silver Lining* 8
A time for everything	*A Song for Every Day* 25
The world is big	*Tinderbox* 33

Prayers

Page 219

ARE YOU NICE TO KNOW?

46 It's not my fault

Theme

If something is your fault, then take the blame.

Let's talk

If you are running in the school and you bump into someone else who is running too, whose fault is it?

If you are running and you bump into someone else who is standing still, whose fault is *that*?

What would you say to that person?

Is that what you *should* say?

Time to listen

We're back in the Beautiful Garden again. This time the story is about Camel.

The Clumsy Camel

Camel was neither a gentle nor a polite creature. She was always treading on something or crashing into someone, and never thought it was her own fault.

One day, she trod on Snail who cried, 'Camel, you are cracking my house!'

Camel replied, 'Serve you right for being in the way. What a fuss to make about a silly shell. You can always grow another one.' But, of course, Snail could not. Snail complained to The Keeper, whose job it was to care for the animals, saying that Camel was always blaming other creatures for being in the way.

The Keeper told Camel that the next time she blamed another animal for her own clumsiness, a small hump would begin to grow on her smooth back. And, every time she blamed someone else after that, the hump would grow a little more.

'Ha!' snorted Camel, 'You must think I am a fool to believe *that*.' The Keeper said nothing but smiled a secret smile. Next day, Camel had a really busy day. She crashed into a Spiky Bush and Parrot and Chimpanzee tumbled to the ground. She bumped into a rock, which rolled down the hill, hitting Rhino on its way.

And, each time, Camel said the accident was not her fault. Sure enough, when she woke up in the morning, what did she find on her back but – a hump. But Camel took no notice – she bashed and crashed and smashed and trod and blamed everyone but herself. By the end of the week, she had a big, lumpy hump upon her back.

And, ever since, every camel has a hump on its back. Some camels even have *two* humps. I wonder why?

The message is

Don't blame everyone else if the fault is yours.

Share you thoughts with everyone

If you do something wrong or silly, do you always take the blame?

Why not? Should you?

Think quietly about

About the times when you have blamed somebody else – and it was your fault all the time!

Songs to sing

Both sides now	*Alleluya* 33
A living song	*Come & Praise* 72
It's a great, great shame	*Every Colour* 44
Dis long time, gal	*Mango Spice* 32
A strange menagerie	*Play School Song Book* 19
Sticky side down	*Silly Aunt Sally* 59

Prayers

Page 219

47 I am the greatest!

Theme

Attitudes of superiority, vulgarly known as being a big-head. A few children in Years 1 and 2 (and beyond ...) tend to regard themselves as being superior to many of their peers, for a variety of reasons.

They may be bigger and stronger, come from more affluent backgrounds or find learning easier than their fellows. We cannot change personalities but perhaps we can attempt limitation of the arrogance factor.

Let's talk

Let us invent a person and call her Lily Pink.

She can read better and run faster than anyone else in the school/department.

She thinks she is a better person than anyone else.

Is she?

Time to listen

This is another story about the Beautiful Garden.

I am a Mole and I live in a Hole

The animals in the Beautiful Garden had been arguing about who would make the best king or queen, and the argument became a chorus of roaring and screeching, and claws and teeth were shown.

So The Keeper decided to call a Great Meeting where they would talk about the idea sensibly and each, if they so wished, would give the reasons why they would be better at being King or Queen than any other animal.

Elephant began by trumpeting, 'I am the biggest animal that lives on earth so I must be King.'

'No, no, no,' hissed Snake, 'I have the most poisonous bite of all so *I* should be Queen.' At that, Mongoose said she could kill Snake in a flash with her sharp teeth, Giraffe said she was the tallest animal of all, Bear said he could fight on two legs but Kangaroo said that so could he, Tortoise said she had a house on her back but so did Turtle and Snail.

Deer said she could run faster than any other animal but Cheetah said, 'That's what you think'. Ostrich boasted that she laid the biggest egg in the world but Chimpanzee said, 'So what?' because most animals did not lay eggs, anyway, so that didn't count.

'Besides,' said Chimpanzee, 'I have a thumb on each hand and I am very clever. Which means *I* should be King.'

'Not if I eat you first,' snarled Leopard, showing his teeth. As he spoke, there was a loud rumbling noise and the ground fell in, making a deep hole. The animals were very frightened.

'This must be a creature mighty enough to be King or Queen of us all,' roared Tiger. Then a little hump appeared in the bottom of the hole and all the animals shivered with fright.

The hump got bigger and burst in a shower of soil and, out of the top, popped the head of a tiny creature with a shiny, black velvet coat and two tiny, button-shiny eyes.

'Hello!' it squeaked, 'I'm Mole. I didn't mean the tunnel to collapse. Sorry to disappoint you but I am not mighty at all and if you think I am, you must all be too stupid for any one of you to become King or Queen – of anything or anywhere. Just forget the whole idea, be yourselves and don't worry about who is the greatest!'

Whereupon, Mole disappeared down the hole before the animals realised what fools they had been.

The message is

Be careful about claiming you are the greatest – you don't know who's out there.

Share your thoughts with everyone

Why do some people think they *are* the greatest?

Think quietly about

Whether you think you are better than other children.

If you do, why?

If you show how you feel, have you any idea what other children think about *you*?

Songs to sing

All the animals	*Come & Praise* 80
Such hard work	*Every Colour* 29
Reach out	*Sing it in the Morning* 22
Sing a song of people	*Tinderbox* 16
The world is big, the world is small	*Tinderbox* 33

Prayers

Page 219

48 No problem!

Theme

Over-confidence.

Let's talk

Do you know any children or grown-ups who claim they can do everything?

Can they really?

Time to listen

Jessica taught her dad a lesson in this story.

Jessica and a Cupboard

'Daddy,' said Jessica, 'What are you doing? I thought we were going skating this afternoon.'

Jo, put down his screwdriver and said, cheerfully, 'Shan't be long, pet. I'll just finishing putting this cupboard together that I bought yesterday. Go and watch tele for a bit, eh?'

Jessica picked up a printed sheet off the floor, waved it at her dad and enquired carefully, 'Don't you need these instructions to make the cupboard?'

Her father smiled and said confidently, 'Oh, no, I don't need instructions. I can do a simple job like this without them. Besides, I've almost finished.' Jessica looked hard at the cupboard and screwed up her face.

'Daddy,' she enquired thoughtfully, 'Are you sure you don't need the instructions?'

Joe began to look irritated and snapped, 'No, I do not. Now let me get on. I've only got the the door handles to fix. Now go and watch tele.'

'Daddy,' said Jessica, speaking very quickly because she could see that her dad was getting very cross, 'Are you sure you haven't made a mistake?'

Joe made a choking noise and snapped, 'Since when have you known more about woodwork than I do? If I say I have not made a mistake then I haven't. Now go away.' Jessica made a beeline for the door.

'Daddy,' said the little girl, ready to beat a hasty retreat, 'If you *have* done it right, where are you going to fix the door handles? Because it looks to me as if you've got the door at the back instead of the front. I can see the keyhole.' Joe looked as if he was about to yell at Jessica. Instead, he looked at his work and his face fell.

'Oh, crikey,' he groaned, 'She's right. So I have. And I've glued it in place.' I'm sorry, ...' But Jessica had gone.

The message is

It does not pay to think you know it all.

Share your thoughts with everyone

Do we always need instructions to do a job?

Are there times when it is essential to have some instructions to do a job?

Can you understand instructions if you are not a good reader?

Are there other ways of getting instructions?

Think quietly about

The times when you have started a job without really knowing the best way of doing it.

Songs to sing

When Father papered the parlour	*Apusskidu* 34
The building song	*Come & Praise* 61

Indeed I would	*Jolly Herring* 5
Can you tell me	*Okki-tokki-unga* 55
You can do it	*Sing a Silver Lining* 9
Work calypso	*Music Box Song Book* 21
	and *Tinderbox* 23

Prayers

Page 219

49 Highest, biggest, longest

Theme

Stretching the truth for effect – exaggeration or the Munchausen syndrome (not the medical condition!).

Let's talk

Who has ever said they have something bigger or better than someone else?

What was it?

Were you being truthful?

Time to listen

Once people start boasting it is hard to stop. The people in this story found that out.

Would You Believe It?

All the chiefs of the tribes of the far-away place called Uplands had come to choose a new King because the ancient King Eno had left to be with the Spirits of the Forests and the Rivers.

Because the Meeting was of great importance, the chiefs had taken along their eldest sons and daughters with them, so that they would know who the next King would be. Before the Choosing began, the young people gathered under a giant Panno tree to eat its sweet fruit. As they ate they began to talk.

'What a huge tree this is,' said the girl Zeta, looking above her head, 'I don't think I have seen bigger even in Farout, my home village.'

'Ha!' snorted the boy Aya, 'In my village, called Wayout, the trees in our forests are so tall that they blot out the sun and we have to carry lamps to find our way about.'

'Oh!' exclaimed the girl Nora, 'That's nothing. In Reachout, my village, the trees grow so tall that their tops make holes in the clouds and down comes the rain. So it rains all the time and our babies are now being born with webbed feet.'

'Huh,' sneered the boy, Ola, 'Our trees are so tall that you cannot see the tops of them even from our highest mountain. Do you know, one day our witch doctor Oldbones climbed one of them to talk to the forest gods and he has never been seen since. Now is that tall or is that tall?'

Then the youngest boy, Alba, of the land called Shortout and who was no more than six summers old, chirped, 'Definitely not as tall as the stories you lot have been telling, I've never heard such rubbish in all my life. You are all telling silly stories. And, what is more, nobody believes any of them. So why tell them at all?' And nobody could think of an answer.

The message is

Saying things are bigger and better than they are is really a waste of time.

Share your thoughts with everyone

Is it true that if you say that things *are* what they are *not*, then are you only fooling yourself?

Is it lying if you boast about how wonderful things are, even if they aren't?

Why do you think people boast like this?

Think quietly about

Making things out to be bigger, better or more expensive than they really are.

Songs to sing

Last night I had the strangest dream	*Alleluya* 45
Tis the gift to be simple	*Come & Praise* 97
The Boaster	*Music Box Song Book* 51
Song for a bragging dragon	*Silly Aunt Sally* 52
Lord, I love to stamp and shout	*Someone's Singing, Lord* 5
You can't keep a horse in a lighthouse	*Ta-ra-ra-boom-de-ay* 23

Prayers

Page 219

50 What a whopper!

Theme

Not telling the truth or, if you prefer, telling lies.

Let's talk

What is the difference between lying and not telling the truth?

Are there times when it is better not to tell the whole truth?

Time to listen

It is not always easy to tell whether somebody is telling the truth or not.

Stranger in the House

'Herman,' tweeted Harriet Hedge Sparrow, who was sitting on her three eggs, 'Come and look at this poor, sad bird.'

Her mate looked down at a lower branch of the tree and chirped, 'Oh, it does look poorly. What kind of bird is it? I've not see a grey bird like that before.'

Harriet said, 'I don't know but it does not look at all well and we must help it.'

She called out to the grey bird that was clinging on to the branch below, 'Hey, grey bird, you don't look well. Can we help you?'

The grey bird cried pitifully, 'Oh, yes, please. I have been attacked by a nasty hawk and it has damaged my wing. May I rest in your nest for a little while before I fly on to my home, which is not far away?'

Herman perched next to the stranger and tweeted, 'Of course, if you can make your way up to our nest.'

The grey stranger fluttered up to the nest, where it flopped down alongside Harriet. No sooner had it arrived than it wriggled and squirmed and chattered away in a bird-language the sparrows did not know. Then, suddenly, it soared out of the nest, making a most peculiar noise.

'I only wanted somewhere to lay my precious egg,' it hooted as it flew away, 'There's nothing wrong with me! Wasn't that a clever lie I told? Look after my egg, you stupid little Hedge Sparrows. Goodbye!'

Harriet looked down at the big brown egg which the strange bird had laid next to her own clutch of pretty blue ones, not quite sure what to do. Then, being a caring little bird and, because that's what birds do, she sat on them all.

Then, one morning a few weeks later, two bewildered Hedge Sparrows woke up to see a very large, grey chick, bigger than they were themselves, throwing their own cheeping chicks out of the nest with its huge beak.

What, of course, the Hedge Sparrows did not know was that the strange chick was … a cuckoo.

The message is

What a pity the lying bird got away with it – this time.

Share your thoughts with everyone

Can people get away with lying all the time?

Is lying a clever thing to do?

Songs to sing

Turn, turn, turn	*Alleluya* 32
The bare necessities	*Sing a Silver Lining* 14
Take the time to cogitate	*Every Colour* 47
It's a new day	*A Song for Every Day* 106
Can anyone tell me that?	*Tinderbox* 6
I went to the cabbages	*Tinderbox* 46

Prayers

Page 219

51 The best policy

Theme

Honesty.

Let's talk

If you found a £5 note on the ground, what would you do?

If you found a purse and it had a name inside it, what would you do?

What *should* you do?

Time to listen

Tinpot soon found out that taking someobody's else's property without asking was a silly thing to do.

Tinpot Learns his Lesson

Long, long ago a wizard called Mayzin had a nephew by the name of Tinpot. Early one morning, Tinpot took a magic stick from his uncle's cave without asking first. He had always wanted such a stick and he told himself that Uncle Mayzin would never know. But we know better, don't we?

When the magic words, 'Zeena Zana Zoona' were said, the stick changed instantly into all sorts of strange things. Tinpot grasped the stick and chanted, 'Zeena Zana Zoona!'

Instantly the stick changed into ... an elephant's trunk without the elephant, a squiggly hosepipe and a giant stick of candy.

Tinpot cried, 'Oozy, Azzy, Eezy!' which were the magic words to stop the stick's antics, and set off to the Long Track to play tricks on travellers.

He laid the stick in the middle of the track and hid behind a thick bush. One by one, along came some travellers, each of whom picked up the stick, intending to take it away with them. But, each time, the stick changed into something unpleasant.

The stick became, in turn, a stupendous, squirming, spitting live sausage, a bag of squiggly, smelly, steaming maggots, a huge, horrible, hairy, horsefly and a disgusting, devilish, dwarf, droning dragon that breathed out smoke and flames. All the terrified travellers ran away yelling or screaming, and Tinpot enjoyed the joke each time, telling himself that all of them had meant to be dishonest and steal the stick. He did not stop to think that he had been more dishonest than any of them had. Then along came Father Oswald, a kind and gentle monk. He saw the stick and was about to pick it up.

'Oh, I must not,' said the holy man, 'The stick belongs to someone else. If I take it, I shall be doing something dishonest. And that is quite wrong.' So he left the stick on the ground.

'Silly old fool,' said Tinpot, after the monk had gone, 'Who was to know that he took the stick? Except me. I think honest people like that are really stupid.' No sooner had he said that than the stick sprang into the air, bounced behind the bush and began to beat him. It continued to beat him until he ran back to Mayzin's cave and put the stick back where he had found it. You may be certain that, after that, Tinpot never did anything dishonest again.

The message is

Do not call someone else dishonest unless you are honest yourself.

Share your thoughts with everyone

Tell me what you know about somebody being dishonest (no names, of course!).

Do you know why that person was dishonest?

How did you feel when you saw it?

Think quietly about

Whether *you* have ever been dishonest and why.

Songs to sing

One more step	*Come & Praise* 47
Because you care	*Every Colour* 31
Seeds of kindness	*Every Colour* 42
Spooky	*Harlequin* 36
How do you feel today?	*Play School Song Book* 1
Let's pretend	*Tinderbox* 25

Prayers

Page 219

*52 Don't miss school

Theme

Absenteeism.

Let's talk

Who enjoys school?

Why do children stay away from school when they do not have any reason to do so?

Why is it important for children not to miss a lot of school?

Time to listen

Going to school matters more than telling others how wonderful you are.

Pansy Piglet and a Tail

Pansy Piglet had a wonderfully curly tail and her mother had tied a pretty blue ribbon on it before Pansy skipped off to school one bright sunny day. Indeed, it was so sunny that she said to herself, 'I'm not going to mouldy old school today. I'll go and show everybody my tail.'

She went to the big oak tree where Spike Squirrel lived in his nest which is called a drey.

She called, 'Spike, would you like to see my lovely curly tail?'

Spike shouted, 'No, I don't! My own tail is all bushy and furry and it doesn't need silly bows on it. Go away!'

Sniffing haughtily, Pansy walked to Acorn Ring and called down the rabbit hole, 'Mrs Rimmy Rabbit, would you like to see my lovely curly tail with a beautiful blue ribbon on it?'

A voice came from deep down the hole, 'No. My tail is all white and fluffy and it doesn't need silly bows on it. Go away!'

A hail of carrot ends whizzed out of the hole so Pansy moved on to Bushy Tump and called into the fox's den, 'Mr Fernando Fox, would you like to see my lovely curly tail with its pretty blue bow?'

Pansy heard a growl, 'No. My tail which is called a brush is all red and bushy and it doesn't need silly bows on it. Now go away!' The fox popped his head out of the hole and showed his sharp teeth, so Pansy ran away.

The next day her friends wanted to know where she had been the day before, because they had all enjoyed a wonderful show by Pooky and his Perky Puppets. Then I am afraid that Pansy did something even worse than staying away from school. She told a big porkie – which I expect you know is the joke name for a lie – to her teacher and to her friends.

She said she stayed in bed with a tail-ache. But as she told this porkie, a dreadful pain went through her tail, just as a tooth hurts with toothache.

Pansy twisted round and saw that her tail had gone completely straight. And, I am sorry to say, that is how it stayed for ever and ever. Not that it had anything to do with staying off school.

The message is

You may not know it but you might miss something really good if you stay off school without a good reason.

Share you thoughts with everyone

Tell me some of the things you could miss if you stayed away from school.

Two proper names can be given to 'staying away from school without a good reason'. Tell me what they are.

What do children call it?(varies from area to area).

Can your parents or your guardians get into trouble if you stay away from school without a good reason?

Think quietly about

How upset your parents or guardians would be if they found out that you were playing truant.

Songs to sing

Turn, turn, turn	*Alleluya* 32
The building song	*Alleluya* 59
Each day different	*Harlequin* 43
The lightning tree	*Jolly Herring* 65
Can you tell me?	*Okki-tokki-unga* 55
One two three	*Tinderbox* 73

Prayers

Page 219

*53 It isn't funny

Theme

Teasing.

Let's talk

What *is* teasing?

Do children being teased enjoy it?

Do children doing the teasing enjoy it? Should they?

Time to listen

There are all sorts of things that can stop children from teasing others.

Simba, Simba

Osomo was not like the other boys in the village. He did not enjoy the mock lion hunts that most of the other boys thought were the best games of all to play.

Osomo hated the idea of throwing toy spears at pretend lions and leopards. He loved all real animals too much even to pretend to kill imaginary ones and, even worse, to enjoy doing it. Osobo liked nothing better than to wander in the forest and watch the baboons making faces at him from the trees, or to watch the sleepy crocodiles as they yawned before sunset over the yellow Chakpani River.

One day, on his way to the forest, Osobo found his way into the forest barred by four boys from the village, who loved the make-believe lion hunts and who could not wait to grow up to take part in the real thing.

From time to tine, all of them had teased Osobo a little about his dislike of hunting, but today it seemed that they were out to make a fool of Osobo and to do some serious teasing.

They began to dance around him, pointing wooden spears at him and chanting 'Osobo is a coward chicken, coward chicken!' as they threw squashy fruit from a pile they had got ready earlier.

But, as Osobo dodged the messy bread-fruit, the tormentors heard a snarl and they turned to see two shining yellow eyes peering from behind a tree. They belonged to a large, hungry-looking lioness. Ikaru, the oldest boy, squealed with fear and he and his brother, Amala, turned to run. The other two boys turned to run after them.

'Stand still,' hissed Osobo, 'Don't move. Keep quiet.' His four shivering tormentors froze to the spot.

Osobo walked firmly towards the growling creature and said, quietly and firmly, 'Go, Simba, go, leave in peace,' he said, 'We shall not harm your babies.' The lion tossed its head, roared softly, and disappeared into the trees.

Do you think that Isobo was ever teased again after that?

The message is

Those who tease others may regret it.

Share your thoughts with everyone

Is teasing a kind of bullying?

If you ever tease another child, would you think of yourself as a bully?

If you are being teased a lot, what should you do about it?

Think quietly about

Whether you have teased anyone without stopping to think that you might be making that person very unhappy.

Songs to sing

Lawrence the lion	*Alphabet Zoo Book* 35
Old Henery the lion	*Multi-Coloured Music Bus* 40
Would you turn your back?	*Every Colour* 34
It's a great, great shame	*Every Colour* 44
I lift my finger	*Ta-ra-ra-boom-de-ay* 39
Don't you push me down	*Tinderbox* 26

Prayers

Page 219

*54 Big and little bullies

Theme

Bullying.

Let's talk

What *is* bullying?

Tell me about some kinds of bullying.

Is it only boys that bully other children?

Time to listen

Not all bullies are big.

You May Think You're Top Dog

'Hey, you nearly trod on me then,' squeaked Cheeky Chihuahua, the smallest dog in the street.

'Ow!' She let out a squeal as Sammy Scottie Dog nipped her tiny back leg, 'Why did you do that? I've done nothing to you.'

Sammy Scottie Dog snarled, 'Look, if I feel like nipping you, I will. I'm bigger than you are are so clear off before I bite you properly.' He trotted off, feeling so pleased with himself that he bumped into Buster Bulldog.

'Watch it, tiddler,' snapped Buster Bulldog, 'Or I shall bite *you*. I'm bigger than you are so just clear off before I bite you properly.' He bared his teeth. Sammy Scottie Dog took one look at them and left in a hurry.

Bulldog stood, wagging his stumpy tail and laughing as he watched Sammy Scottie Dog disappear up the road. He was wagging his tail so much that he flicked Rosie Rottweiler in the eye.

Now, many of you will know that a Rottweiler is a very big dog with big teeth, and other dogs do their best not to annoy her.

'Hey, watch what you're doing with that silly little tail of yours,' growled Rosie Rottweiler, 'Just take care or else I shall show you what a real bite is and you won't have even have a stumpy tail any more. I'm bigger than you, so push off before I remove your leg as well.'

Buster Bulldog scurried off as fast as his short legs would carry him.

'Ho ho,' said Rosie Rottweiler to herself, 'I enjoyed that.' Then, suddenly, she let out a howl and rushed off up the street, twisting and turning and jumping and hopping and scratching and scratching and scratching. She made such a noise that she woke old Basil Basset Hound.

'What's the matter with her?' asked Cheeky Chihuahua.

Basil Basset Hound yawned and sniggered, 'It's Ferdinand Flea looking for a dog to bite so that he can have his dinner,' he sniggered, 'And I think he has found one. That will teach big bully Rosie Rottweiler that there's always someone who can play the same game of bullying others. Only that someone doesn't have to be bigger!' And he went back to sleep.

The message is

Bullies often get what's coming to them.

Share your thoughts with everyone

Should you ever let bullies get away with their nasty habit?

Is it wise to try to stick it out?

Is it wise to try and fight it by yourself?

What should you do?

Think quietly about

Doing something about it if you are being bullied.

Making up your mind never to be a bully yourself.

Songs to sing

I whistle a happy tune	*Apusskidu* 3
Raindrops keep falling on my head	*Alleluya* 58
You can build a wall(Break out)	*Come & Praise* 91
I am planting my feet	*Come & Praise* 103
We want to sing	*Sing a Silver Lining* 7
Don't you push me down	*Tinderbox* 26

Prayers

Page 219

55 Once made, never broken

Theme

Keeping promises once they have been made.

Let's talk

What is a promise?

Tell me some kinds of promises that people make.

Do they aways keep them?

Time to listen

Promises are not made to be broken later.

You May Have Meant it but …

Tomos was a fisherman whose fishing boat was badly damaged in a collision. The ship builder mended it and tied it up in the harbour for the night. But sad to say, a storm swept the boat away and Tomos did not know what to do.

He wailed, 'How can I feed my family if I have no fish to sell?' Then Tomos felt a gentle tap on his shoulder and turned to see an old man with long white hair and a long white beard standing at his side.

'I shall help you, Tomos, said the old man kindly, 'All you need do is to promise to meet me here, in ten years time, with a basket of ten shining, silver fish.' Tomos thought this strange but agreed, as he had nothing to lose. The old man pointed out to sea and to his amazement, Tomos saw, bobbing gently on the tide – his little boat. Lucky Tomos went to sea again and landed huge catches of fish.

He became so rich that, after a year, he had a fleet of fifty boats. Tomos became an important man in the town and forgot all about his promise to the old man. Until the morning there was a knock on his door and there stood an the very same old man. A servant showed him into Tomos' office.

'Where are my ten fish, Tomos, you foolish man?' he asked, sadly, 'You have broken your word to me, Neptune, Lord of the Sea!' As Tomos looked, the old man with white hair and beard disappeared and, in his place, a green giant with the tail of a fish sat on a seaweed-covered throne. He wore a crown and held a three-pointed spear called a trident in one hand. Then he, too, vanished and Tomos wondered if he had been dreaming.

As he thought about it, the captain of one of his ships who came to tell him that every one of his ships had sunk in a fearful hurricane. Tomos was a rich man no longer.

It was then that he realised that it was breaking his promise that had brought misfortune upon him.

The message is

Breaking a promise is not always so serious but it could cause you and other people a lot of trouble.

Share your thoughts with everyone

If you make a promise what should you do?

If you make a promise and you know you cannot keep it, what should you do?

If you have made a promise and did not keep it, what should you do?

Think quietly about

The times *you* have made a promise and not tried to keep it.

Whether it is better to make a promise and break it or not to make one at all.

Songs to sing

Both sides now	*Alleluya* 33
On life's highway	*Every Colour* 28
I jump out of bed in the morning	*Okki-tokki-unga* 47
Try again	*Music Box Song Book* 26
Think, think, on these things	*Someone's Singing, Lord* 38
You and I	*Tinderbox* 55

Prayers

Page 219

THE PLACE WHERE WE LIVE

56 Bin it!

Theme

Dropping litter.

Let's talk

Imagine you have been given an iced lolly by someone.

You take off the wrapper and … finish the sentence for me (Asssume an answer of 'Put it in the bin).

Why should you do that?

Give me the names of some kinds of litter.

Time to listen

This was a strange way to be given a lesson on disposing of litter – but it worked for Larry!

Larry and The Litterbug

Larry is a well-behaved, kind and polite boy. Unfortunately, Larry is also the untidiest boy I have ever known. If he bought anything that had a wrapper or came in a can, he never, ever, put the wrapper or the can in a litter-bin.

One day at the park, he opened a can of fizzy orange drink, drank it and threw the can on the grass. Then he settled down to read his comic. After a while, he felt sleepy and, strangely, found himself walking in the warm sunshine along the street to his house.

As he walked along, he heard a tiny, squeaky voice, 'Oi, you boy! I'm talking to you!' Larry whizzed round. All he could see was a bright orange can in the middle of the footpath.

It was a very strange can with tiny arms and legs, two bright eyes and a mouth, which was the hole in the top.

Larry said out loud, feeling quite scared, 'This is silly.'

'What is?' asked the can.

'This is. Whoever heard of a can talking?' squawked Larry, walking on a little faster. He turned to look behind him and, sure enough the can was following him. Larry started to run. So did the can. When Larry got indoors, the can was sitting on the settee. It was on the table when he sat down for tea, in the bath when Larry went to clean his teeth and asleep on his pillow when he went to bed.

He picked up the can and threw it to the other side of the room, where it bounced off the wall and straight back on to the pillow. Then the can started giggling, so much that the bed began to shake and went on shaking.

As the bed shook, Larry heard a soft voice, 'Come on, lad, I want to cut the grass.' The boy opened his eyes. A man in green overalls was shaking him gently.

'Wake up and get up,' said the man, laughing, 'I must cut the grass. And while you're at it, will you pick up that orange can that some untidy person threw down? Thanks.'

I wonder if Larry dropped litter again?

The message is

Of course, there are no talking cans but you should be like Larry is now – and never drop litter. But you never do, do you?

Share your thoughts with everyone

Instead of throwing away bottles, cans and paper, can we do anything useful with them?

(The desired response is, of course, *recycling*, although the actual word may not be forthcoming. It is up to you how you develop this line, but it will probably be more appropriate in the classroom/teaching unit situation.)

Think quietly about

Whether you put your litter in the proper place.

Songs to sing

I'm going to paint	*Come & Praise* 83
Keep the countryside tidy	*Every Colour* 14
Across the hills	*Jolly Herring* 17
The Dustbin Man	*Silly Aunt Sally* 67
Milk bottle tops and paper bags	*Someone's Singing, Lord* 17
The Tidy Song	*Tinderbox* 47

Prayers

Page 220

57 Paper is better

Theme

Graffiti.

Let's talk

Who likes to see walls covered with patterns and pictures made with spray-cans?

Whu usually does this spraying?

Do you think it should be allowed?

Time to listen

Bobkin Bumble, the little Brockle, gets himself in trouble – once again!

The Cup Final

Bobkin Bumble, a Brockle of whom you may have heard before, often does some naughty things. Some of them are in his school which is called Butter Meadow. One afternoon, he turned the school clock forward an hour and the whole school went home early, and then there was the time ... oh, but I really haven't got time to tell you about all the silly things that he does. I will tell you that he is not allowed out to play very often

... . But what he did last week was sillier than usual. Bobkin had been picked to play in Butter Meadow School football team in the Cup Final against Foxglove Woods School. So he decided to tell everybody who lived in Brockleton that his school was bound to win the Cup.

Bobkin wanted everyone to know that his team were going to win, so with his felt pens he scribbled 'Butter Meadow for the Cup – We are the Greatest!' – everywhere! And I mean everywhere. All over the window of the village shop, on Benny Banani's ice-cream vans, on Farmer Bumper's best cow Booboo, on the wall round Miss Beebit's cottage ... and that was where Bobkin made his mistake. Because she is the Headteacher of Butter Meadow School and she caught him doing it.

She did not allow Bobkin to play in the Cup Final and Butter Meadow School lost the Cup Final by 15 goals to none. Of course, Bobkin being Bobkin, he went around telling people that they would probably have won if he had been playing. Not that anyone believed him.

The message is

If you think you are an artist, then do your art in the right place – on paper.

Share your thoughts with everyone

It is usually older boys and young men who spray pictures and patterns where they are not supposed to.

Would you like to do it when you are older?

Or is there a better way of showing how good you are with paints?

Think quietly about

Whether scribbling or drawing, where you are not supposed to, makes the place look any better.

Songs to sing

Sing a rainbow	*Apusskidu* 5
Paintbox	*Harlequin* 32
The world is such a lovely place	*Every Colour* 8
I'm going to paint	*Come & Praise* 83
Green lanes	*Jolly Herring* 41
Place to be	*Tinderbox* 34

Prayers

Page 200

58 What fun?

Theme

Vandalism.

Children at Key Stage 1 do not, as a rule, indulge in the same kind of vandalism as older children and young adults. At the same time, it is worth our while to point out the undesirability of wanton destruction for pleasure.

Let's talk

Some people, children and young grown-ups like to break and damage all kinds of things like young trees, street lights, signposts and so on.

If you have ever seen damage like this, tell us about it.

Does it make you feel angry?

Or don't you care?

Time to listen

You would not expect gods of long ago to enjoy breaking things just for fun.

Heavenly Vandals

Long, long ago, the people called the Ancient Greeks believed in many gods, each one in charge of something to do with the world, such as a god of rivers, a god of fire or a god of the sun.

One day, Helios, god of the sun, was talking to Aeolus, chief god of the winds, as they sat eating juicy grapes. Aeolus had left his home on a floating island and was visiting Mount Olympus, where most of the gods lived.

As they talked, along came Eris, a goddess who loved to stir up trouble. Laughing, she told Aeolus that he must be very strong – perhaps the most powerful god of all after Zeus, the mightiest god of all, and she went on her way, having made them think bad thoughts.

'Nonsense,' boasted Helios, pointing to a field of corn far below the mountain, 'I am so powerful that I can burn that corn to cinders. You couldn't!' He puffed at the corn for a second and it burst into flames, leaving nothing but black smuts.

'Ha!', sneered Aeolus, 'I can blow away what you can only scorch. Watch me!' He blew and every tree in the woods was swept away. After that, the two boastful gods burnt or blew away three farms, six woods, ten fields of corn and a temple.

The temple had just collapsed when Pan, the powerful god of all Nature appeared and spoke angrily to them, 'What have you done, to use your godly power so wickedly? I tell you that, one day, mortals who destroy beautiful and useful things for their own pleasure. as you have done, will be called *vandals*. That makes you godly vandals and you should be ashamed. Begone with you and mend your destruction. Or else I shall tell Zeus and you will be punished!'

Helios and Aeolus realised what they had done and were sorry. Happily, they did as Pan said and they never did anything so stupid again.

The message is

The damage done by to things by thoughtless people is called vandalism.

Share your thoughts with everyone

Can you give any reason why people should want to be vandals?

Would you enjoy being a vandal?

Why?

Think quietly about

Any time when you have broken something just because you felt like it.

Whether that made you a vandal.

Songs to sing

The world is such a lovely place	*Every Colour* 8
There's so much pleasure	*Every Colour* 10
Can you hear	*Harlequin* 33
Across the hills	*Jolly Herring* 18
The gift of water	*Sing it in the Morning* 53
On a wonderful day like today	*Sing a Silver Lining* 8

Prayers

Page 220

FAMILY OF NATURE

59 Matthew and the Nashtumtums

Let's talk

Who has a garden at home?

What is grown in it?

Who looks after it?

Where do flowers come from?

Where does fruit come from?

Time to listen

If you plant seeds you must look after them.

Matthew Learns about Seeds

'What seeds are you planting, Grandad?' said three-year old Matthew. He was watching his grandfather making little holes in the brown, crumbly soil of his garden with a piece of pointed wood, called a 'dibber'. Grandad loved his garden which was full of pretty flowers and healthy vegetables.

'I'm planting nasturtium seeds,' he said, smiling, 'Do you like nasturtiums?'

'I dunno,' said a puzzled Matthew, 'What's nashtumtums?'

Grandad laughed, 'Oh, they're red and yellow and orange flowers with strong-smelling leaves. Some people eat the leaves in salads.'

'Well then, please can I have some nashtumtum seeds to grow?' asked the little boy. Grandad gave him six fat nasturtium seeds. When he got home, Matthew made holes in the soil with his own dibber, an old pencil, just like Grandad had done and popped in the seeds.

All the following week, he kept watching but nothing happened. The next time he went see Grandad again, he was annoyed to see that

Grandad's nasturtium seeds had tiny leaves on them.

'Why aren't my nashtumtum seeds sprouting like yours, Grandad?' asked Matthew.

Grandad asked, 'Have you watered them?' The little boy shook his head. Of course, Grandad told him that this was why they were not sprouting. So, when Matthew went home he used Dad's watering-can to spray water all over the soil where he had sown his seeds.

In three days time, they came up and began to grow quite big. Then, one morning, Matthew went out to look at his nasturtiums and ... they had almost disappeared. They had been eaten by hungry caterpillars or it might have been slugs. Of course, Matthew was very disappointed.

'I'm fed up with growing seeds, Grandad,' he said, 'Nothing seems to go right.'

'Tell you what,' said Grandad, seeing Matthew's miserable face, 'Let's try again. And this time, we will have to make sure they don't become slugs' or caterpillars' dinners. I'll sow your seeds in special soil, called compost, in a plastic plant pot and you can put them on a shelf where the slugs can't get at them.'

Matthew thought that was a brilliant idea. He took the pot and soil home and sowed the six new seeds that Grandad had given him and put the pot on a shelf near the window in his Dad's shed out of the reach of slugs and caterpillars.

This time, he watered them every other day and they grew into healthy plants. In a few weeks, pretty red and yellow and orange flowers appeared on them, which made Matthew one very happy boy. Success at last!

The message is

You need to know a lot to be a good gardener and there is always something new to learn.

Share your thoughts with everyone

What else besides watering is needed for seeds to grow?

Can we use anything other than seeds if we want to grow plants?

Songs to sing

Kisnay baniya poo lan ko
(Who made the flowers red and white?) *Every Colour* 13
Poppies dance in the cornfield *Harlequin* 29

Leave them a flower	*Jolly Herring* 7
Lay my white cloak	*Come & Praise* 112
All things that live below the sky	*Someone's Singing, Lord* 41
Let it be	*Tinderbox* 48

Prayers

Page 220

60 The finest flower

Let's talk

Tell me the names of some flowers that grow from seeds.

Tell me the names of some flowers that grow from bulbs.

Tell me the names of some wild flowers.

Time to listen

Matthew is not in this story – which imagines that flowers can talk.

Flower Talk

If Matthew's Grandad could understand flower talk – I don't think people can, really – he might have heard the flowers in his biggest flower bed talking among themselves. Actually, they were not just talking – they were arguing about who was the prettiest flower and who had the sweetest scent. Rose had started the argument by saying that Dandelion was a nuisance and that she should not have been in the flower border because she was a horrid *weed*! Unlike herself, of course.

Dandelion was very upset and cried, 'I am not a weed, I am a wild flower. Besides, I don't have horrible prickles like you do.'

Bluebell leaned over to Dandelion, jingled her pretty blue flowers and said nastily, 'You may say you are a wild flower but you *smell* awful. You really have no business to be in a smart flower bed like ours.'

Geranium shook her leaves and flowers at Bluebell and shrilled, in a flowery sort of way, 'You smell as bad as Dandelion and *you* are really a wild flower, anyway.'

Zinnia leaned over and flower-laughed, 'You've got a nerve, Geranium. You don't smell – you stink! So who are you to tell other flowers that you are something special?'

And so the argument went on – Lupin said most of the flowers were a boring shape, Sweet Pea said that only clever flowers like her could climb, Pansy announced that she flowered in winter and summer and the Nasturtiums – Matthew's Nashtumtums – sneered that they were about the only flower whose leaves could be eaten by humans without them being poisoned. Cabbages didn't count because they were vegetables.

'Oh, do be quiet,' groaned Snail, who was trying to get some sleep under a dock leaf, 'This is a silly argument. Have you all forgotten what flowers are *really* for? If plants had no flowers they would have no seeds after you flowers have frizzled up and dropped off.' Which made the flowers stop chattering and think about what Snail had said – then they went very, very quiet.

The message is

What a wise Snail! So have *you* ever thought where seeds come from?

Share your thoughts with everone

Who has a favourite flower?

Where can we find flowers used to make a place more beautiful?

Tell me some times when flowers are important.

Songs to sing

Katie's garden	*Apusskidu* 50
Think of a world	*Come & Praise* 17
In the garden	*Every Colour* 23
Paintbox	*Harlequin* 32
In an English country	*Harlequin* 22
All the flowers are waking	*Someone's Singing, Lord* 48

Prayers

Page 220

61 Matthew and the vegetables

Theme

Vegetables don't come from supermarkets.

Let's talk

Who goes shopping with a grown-up?

Do you buy vegetables?

Tell us about them.

Time to listen

So do vegetables come from cans?

Matthew and some Beans

'Grandad,' said Matthew – we're getting to know him, aren't we? – 'Does Grandma know you are burying her potatoes?'

Grandad grinned and picked up a potato and said, 'These aren't Grandma's potatoes. This is a *seed* potato.'

Matthew looked puzzled and said, 'Seed *potatoes*? They won't grow like those nashtumtum seeds like you gave me and the caterpillars and slugs ate, will they?'

Grandad nodded and smiled, 'Oh, yes. I am planting them so that more potatoes will grow under the ground. Next spring I shall be digging up lovely new potatoes for us to eat. I'm going to sow seed for carrots and onions and beetroot, too and other sorts of vegetables.'

Matthew screwed up his face and said, 'Vengentables come from the supermarket. I know 'cos I've seen them there.'

Grandad shook his head and his grandson scowled. He did not like being told he was wrong, but then he is only three.

Grandad said, smiling, 'Yes, but farmers have to grow the vegetables before they get to the supermarket. They don't just appear by magic on the shelves or in cans or in the freezers.'

Matthew went very quiet for a minute or two.

Then he said, thoughtfully,' Grandad do you sow seeds for beans?' His grandfather said that he did.

The little boy asked, 'Well, how do you get them to come up cooked and in cans? Do you sow can seeds as well?' But his Grandad was laughing so much he could not answer. Perhaps you could explain to Matthew?

The message is

You know that vegetables have to be grown first, before they get to the shops.

Share your thoughts with everyone

Tell me the names of some vegetables.

Which vegetables do you like eating?

Tell me some places where we can get vegetables which are not frozen or in cans.

Is it hard work growing vegetables?

Songs to sing

One potato, two potatoes	*Apusskidu* 31
Harvest	*Harlequin* 31
If it wasn't for the 'ouses in between	*Jolly Herring* 43
In the early morning	*Someone's Singing, Lord* 49
I went to the cabbages	*Tinderbox* 46
Gardens	*Tinderbox* 55

Prayers

Page 220

62 Matthew and trees

Let's talk

Tell me the names of some trees.

Where have you seen them?

Time to listen

Do we ever stop to think about trees?

Matthew Notices Trees

I hope you are not tired of hearing about three-year old Matthew, because I've got another story for you.

His grandfather had taken him out for a walk one day and Matthew had just noticed – as three-year olds do – trees. Have *you* ever really looked at trees and wondered about them?

'Grandad,' said Matthew. Grandad groaned, silently of course, because he would never upset his grandson, and got ready for the questions.

'Why do we have trees?' asked the little boy.

Grandad thought for a minute, then said, slowly, 'Trees are, well, they just *are*...'

Matthew screwed up his face and said, 'Yes, but what they *for*, Grandad?'

'Well, some trees are cut down so we can cut them up,' laughed Grandad. Matthew thought that was very funny and laughed heartily.

Grandad went on, 'We cut up the tree trunks for their wood. Then the wood is made into all sorts of things like fences, and sheds and logs for the fire.'

Excitedly, Matthew interrupted, 'And fur ... fur ... tables and chairs and benches and stools and all sorts of stuff!'

Grandad smiled and said, 'Yes, but who else uses trees besides people?'

The little boy thought hard for a minute, then said brightly, 'I know. Birds and squirrels live in them and woodpeckers peck them.'

''What a clever boy!' cried Grandad, And can you tell me what else people get from trees, besides wood?' But Matthew couldn't tell him – can you tell *me*?

The message is

Trees are not just for looking at.

Share your thoughts with everyone

Tell me about some of the things which are made from wood.

What is sometimes used to make things instead of wood?

Is it better than wood? Or not as good?

Songs to sing

O Christmas Tree	*Carol, Gaily Carol* 41
Pussy Willow	*Harlequin* 12
I can see cherries	*Harlequin* 30
The lightning tree	*Jolly Herring* 73
'Neath the lilacs	*Okki-tokki-unga* 16
Who has seen the wind	*Tinderbox* 44

Prayers

Page 220

PEOPLE WHO LOOK AFTER US

63 A good servant

Theme

Fire and fire prevention.

Let's talk

Tell me some ways in which fire can be started.

Tell me some uses for fire.

Time to listen

Some good things can come out of a bad happening.

This story is based on an old, traditional folk tale about the discovery of roast pork, but, as a concession to possible children's sensitivities, the story has gone vegetarian.

Jackets

Potatoes were first eaten in America, but people ate them raw because they had not discovered how to cook them. One of the people who grew potatoes and ate them raw was a man called Sharni.

One day, he went to the village medicine man, Kanwa, with a tummy-ache that would not go away. Kanwa felt his tummy and looked into his mouth.

The medicine-man said, 'Ah! You are having this tummy-ache because you are not chewing your food properly. All your rotten teeth must be pulled out.' Out came Kanwa's dentist tools and out came Sharni's dreadful teeth. Sure enough, within two weeks, his tummy-ache went away but, because he had no teeth, he had to live on soup and corn porridge.

This meant that Sharni's good crop of potatoes was of no use to him because he could not chew them. So he dug them up, washed them and stored them in clay pots in the bedroom of his hut until someone would buy them from him.

But, one day, a spark from a cooking fire landed on the grass roof of Sharni's little house and soon the whole house was ablaze. When the fire had been put out, Sharni went in to clear away what he thought would be a mess of charred potatoes. But the pots had stopped the potatoes from burning and, instead, a lovely, mouth-watering smell was coming from them.

Sharni broke open one of the hot potatoes and tasted it. It tasted absolutely delicious and it was so soft that it melted away in his toothless mouth. Sharni had disovered jacket potatoes!

The message is

You must not take risks with fire but it is very useful.

Share your thoughts with everyone

Tell me some ways in which people can be careless about fire.

Who should we call if a fire starts at home?

What should we do if a fire starts at school?

Think quietly about

The people whose job is to put out fires.

Songs to sing

One potato, two potatoes	*Apusskidu* 31
The fireman	*Apusskidu* 33
We will take care of you	*Every Colour* 36
Oh, Mister Policeman	*Silly Aunt Sally* 64
A time for everything	*Songs for Every Day* 25
The world is big	*Tinderbox* 33

Prayers

Page 221

64 Emergency or not?

Theme

Telephoning 999 – but is it an emergency?

Let's talk

Who knows what to do if there is an accident *in school.*

Who knows what to do if there is an accident *at home.*

Time to listen

This is based on a true story.

Emergency! Rabbit in Trouble!

Rosie Rabbit was a tame white rabbit belonging to seven-year old Diana. The bunny lived happily in a comfortable hutch that stood in a little patch of garden, with a fence round it. There, she could nibble the grass and look at the blue sky.

Rosie had a wild rabbit friend called Rowena. Rowena used to come and visit Rosie when it was dark and they often enjoyed a chat. One night, she asked Rosie what it was like to live in a hutch.

'I've never lived in anything else and it's fine,' laughed Rosie, 'The only time I don't like it is when Foxy Ferdy comes sniffing around and makes me nervous.'

Rowena said, 'Why don't you escape and dig your own burrow. If Foxy is around, you just pop underground.'

Rosie thought about it and next morning, she thought she would practise digging a burrow in her own garden. She scrabbled away and soon had made a long tunnel, about two metres long. The little rabbit was pleased with herself, but decided she preferred her cosy hutch to the dark tunnel. But, when she tried to turn round and get out, she couldn't! She was stuck!

Poor Rosie had discovered that rabbits cannot back out of tunnels – they must turn round first. Neither did she know that wild rabbits always dig a room at the end of the tunnel, big enough to be able to turn round and get out.

When Diana came home from school, she thought Rosie *had* escaped but then she saw the tunnel and realised what had happened. When her parents arrived home, they all tried to rescue Rosie but, try as they might, they could not get the terrified rabbit out of the burrow.

Then her Mum had the bright idea of phoning the police. She rang 999, the number you have to phone in case of emergency.

She knew this was not a real emergency but Sergeant Stamp knew someone in the RSPCA, the people who help animals that are in trouble. It only took the RSPCA officer twenty minutes, using special tools, to pull a very dirty, scared rabbit out of the tunnel, so everybody was happy. Especially Rosie. And you try telling her it wasn't an emergency!

The message is

Make sure you only ring 999 for a real emergency.

Share your thoughts with everyone

Tell me how you would call for an ambulance.

Think quietly about

The wonderful work done by ambulance crews and paramedics.

Songs to sing

Ruskin the Rabbit	*Alphabet Zoo Book* 52
Rabbit ain't got	*Apusskidu* 57
All the animals	*Come & Praise* 80
Oh, Mister Policeman	*Silly Aunt Sally* 64
Telephone song	*Silly Aunt Sally* 87
Jennifer's rabbit	*Tinderbox* 14

Prayers

Page 221

65 Medical matters

Theme

Doctors.

Let's talk

Who can tell me the name of your doctor?

Who does not like doctors?

Why?

Time to listen

Arthur has the wrong idea about doctors – do you?

A Bad Case of Something-or-other

'Mum,' moaned Arthur Bumble, aged ten.

'Now what's wrong?' his mother called up the stairs. She sounded annoyed, 'It was your stomach hurting you last night. What is it this time?'

'I've got an awful headache,' groaned Arthur, 'I can't possibly go to school today. And I was so looking forward to the first swimming lesson in the big pool at Nashchester.'

Mrs Bumble grinned to herself as she came into the bedroom – just as she had thought, Arthur was fibbing – he hated swimming.

'I want to go, Mum, but my head is so bad I think I might die,' he moaned, crossing his fingers under the bedclothes because he knew he was telling a fib.

Mother felt his head. 'Oh, goodness,' she said, shaking her head, 'You *are* hot. I had better think call Doctor Flowse,' and off she went.

Arthur sat up in bed, horrified. What he had let himself in for? He buried his head under the bedclothes and dropped off to sleep. Two hours later he was awakened by voices downstairs. Then he heard footsteps on the stairs.

Doctor Flowse popped his head round the door and grinned at Arthur, whose frightened face was peeping over his duvet.

'Hello, Arthur,' he said, with a little grin, and stuck a thermometer in the boy's mouth He listened to Arthur's chest with a cold thing called a stethoscope and prodded his stomach with ice-cold hands.

'Mm,' said the doctor, 'A bad case of splashitis. It is not serious but I shall have to give you some large, extra strong pills. No TV for three days and you must stay in bed. Nothing to eat today. Perhaps some watery porridge without sugar for breakfast tomorrow. Goodbye, Arthur. I won't need to come back. You will soon feel better.' And off he went, shaking his head and trying not to laugh.

Soon after he had gone, Mrs Bumble came upstairs with two huge pink pills, Arthur suddenly felt better but his Mum made him take them all the same. He had no dinner, either, but Mum felt sorry for him and gave him eggs for breakfast next morning.

Of course, the doctor knew there was nothing wrong with Arthur and the pills were made of sugar. Arthur went swimming the following week without making a fuss. And, do you know, he enjoyed every minute of it?

The message is

Doctors usually know when you are really ill.

Share your thoughts with everyone

When should you see a doctor?

Is there any need to be afraid of a doctor?

Think quietly about

How hard doctors have to work.

Whether you have made a fuss about seeing a doctor when you have been really poorly.

Songs to sing

One man's hands	*Alleluya* 61
Such hard work	*Every Colour* 29
Why does it have to be me?	*Music Box Song Book* 31
Can you tell me?	*Okki-tokki-unga* 55
Let's pretend	*Tinderbox* 25

Prayers

Page 221

66 More medical matters

Theme

Nurses.

Let's talk

Why do children (and grown-ups) sometimes have injections?

Time to listen

Nobody likes injections, but ...

Jabs

'Come along, Jenny,' called Mrs Rankin, 'Time to go. Our appointment for injections is at three o'clock. We must go or there will be no holiday in Egypt.'

Seven-year old Jenny burst into tears and bellowed, 'I don't wanna have a needle stuck in me! It hurts! Don't wanna go to Egypt! Wanna go to Brighton! You don't need 'jections for there.'

Mrs Rankin said, quite calmly, 'Your Daddy has paid out a lot of money for this trip. And we are going. So that's that.'

Jenny realised that there was no escape, so she followed her mother to the Health Centre, still sniffling. Her mother had to promise her a chocolate ice cream *and* a comic before Jenny would let go of the door handle of the Nurses' Room.

Once inside, Nurse Watson said, 'Come along, then. It won't hurt a bit. She picked up a syringe (you know, the thing that has the needle on it) and said, 'Off to Egypt, are you? My, what a lucky girl.' Jenny took one look the syringe and began to howl again and curled up into a ball.

'I'll tell you what, Jenny,' said Nurse, 'Why don't you give my dolly an injection and I will watch you.' She produced a soft, plastic, baby doll and a toy syringe from a cupboard. After filling the syringe with water, she told Jenny to stick the needle into the baby's bottom.

'Oo,' squealed Jenny, 'Dollies can't feel anything, can they? So it won't hurt, will it?' She bent over the doll and did as the nurse said. The next thing she knew was that the nurse was putting a little plaster on her arm.

'Neither did that, did it?' chuckled the nurse.

'What do you mean? Why are you putting that plaster on my arm?' said a puzzled Jenny.

'That's to make sure your injection stays clean,' laughed Nurse Watson.

Jenny squeaked, 'When are you going to do the 'jection, then?'

'I've done it,' laughed the nurse, 'Close your mouth, Jenny, you might swallow a fly!' The little girl could not believe it – she hadn't felt a thing.

Her Mummy told her, as she ate her promised ice cream, 'That injection didn't hurt, because nurses know exactly what to do, especially with awkward children like you.' And Jenny didn't argue about *that*.

The message is

There is no need to make a fuss about injections – they don't really hurt.

Share your thoughts with everyone

If you have ever been in hospital, were the nurses kind to you?

Tell me about some kinds of nurses.

Think quietly about

Whether you would ever like to be a nurse (boys as well as girls).

Songs to sing

Somebody greater	*Come & Praise* 5
Because you care	*Every Colour* 31
Indeed I would	*Jolly Herring* 7
Reach out	*Sing it in the Morning* 22
Miss Polly	*Okki-tokki-unga* 17
Work calypso	*Tinderbox* 23

Prayers

Page 221

*67 An important job

Theme

Binmen and their work.

This assembly has been designated as a sensitive topic because children do have binmen as fathers or guardians and we must be careful not to denigrate the important function that refuse collectors play in keeping the environment clean and healthy.

Let's talk

Tell me some ways in which rubbish or refuse is collected.

Is it a hard job?

Why?

Does anyone know a binman/refuse-collector?

Would he (it is usually a man) come and talk to us about the job?

Time to listen

Percy Pickle was very grateful to the binmen who collected his refuse!

The Careful Binmen

Percy Pickle drank the last of his breakfast coffee and remarked, 'Those binmen are noisy with the bins today. It is usually Lucy who is extra noisy when I have a day off. What *is* she doing?'

'Tidying the bookcase in the living room and throwing out all the old books,' said his wife, Sonia. I am tired of dusting them. Nobody ever reads them, anyway. Why, Percy, whatever is the matter?' Mr Pickle had leapt to his feet, a horrified expression on his face.

'Has she … has she … thrown out *all* the old books?' he gasped and rushed into the living room. The only books left in the bookcase were three Enid Blyton books!

'Lucy, where are the books?' he screeched.

His daughter said, 'I've thrown them out. Aren't you pleased?' They were all old and tatty.' Percy let out a howl and rushed out of the house. Mrs Pickle and Lucy watched him talking to the binmen and waving his arms about, wondering whatever was wrong. Five minutes later he staggered back, clutching a bundle of five large books and collapsed into his armchair.

'Oh, the binmen are so sharp-eyed!' puffed Percy, 'One of them called Jason spotted the books when he opened the lid of the bin, which had our house number on it. He was going to come back before they moved on and ask us if we meant to dump them. He said it was a shame to throw away good books like those and, besides that, they looked as if they might be worth a lot of money to someone. He was right, too, because they are.'

Well, why are they so special and just how much are they worth?' asked Sonia. 'And where did they come from?'

Percy announced proudly, 'They are what we call first editions of books. Books by Charles Dickens.'

The family's eyes popped as Percy said, grinning widely, 'I paid £1 for them at the Boot Sale last week and they are worth ... are you ready for this? About £3000. I was going to tell you tonight.'

'Gosh, wasn't it lucky that the binman had his wits about him?' said Lucy.

'Yes, 'said Percy, 'And even luckier that he recognised good books when he saw them. I shall give him £100 when I sell the books. As for the rest of the money – well, I believe Disneyland is worth a visit.' And nobody argued about *that*!

The message is

Binmen have a most important job – we would be in an awful mess if they did not do their jobs properly.

Share your thoughts with everyone

What would happen if we had no binmen?

What happens to our rubbish after the binmen have collected it?

Think quietly about

People who do unpleasant jobs that *must* be done.

Songs to sing

Pollution Calypso	*Every Colour* 15
Across the hills	*Jolly Herring* 18

The dustbin man *Silly Aunt Sally* 67
Any old iron *Ta-ra-ra-boom-de-ay* 4
We want to sing *Sing a Silver Lining* 8
Sing a song of people *Tinderbox* 37

Prayers
Page 221

68 Where *do* teachers come from?

Theme

Teachers.

Let's talk

How do you think I became a teacher?

Where did I have to go to learn how to teach?

Did I have to go there for long?

Time to listen

Note: You may have to explain to children what a supply teacher is, although most of Key Stage 1 children will understand. They should all know what a robot is.

How would you like a teacher like Rizzie?

The Tin Teacher

The children in Class Z were very badly behaved and it was no wonder that the latest supply teacher had only stayed for an hour. Don't ask me what naughty things they did, because you would not want to know.

But they could not be left without a teacher, so Mrs Wagstaff, the Head Teacher of St Griff's school, had to teach Class Z herself. Class Z did not like that very much. Neither did Mrs Wagstaff.

After lunch she went into her room to do the things that Head Teachers have to do. To her surprise, standing by the window was a strange dustbin-shaped object, as tall as she was. It was buzzing away quietly and a winking red light, that seemed to be its only eye, glowed from its black-and-red striped body.

Mrs Wagstaff was even more surprised when it extended an arm that looked like a long metal whip and said in a scratchy, droning voice, 'I am the answer to your problems. I am Rizzie the Robot Teacher and I have come to take over Class Z for as long as you like.'

And off it trundled, before Mrs Wagstaff could say a word, squeaking and rattling on its ten wheels as it went. Not sure of what was going to happen, she followed the weird machine and looked through the window at Class Z.

The classroom was silent, except for a buzzing sound from the robot teacher as its top half revolved slowly. Every boy and girl was scribbling away like mad, doing very hard sums that were on the blackboard.

Mrs Wagstaff was not pleased to see that they looked very frightened. She did not like the idea of a robot frightening children in her school. As the Head Teacher, she would have to do something about this and that meant going into the classroom, robot or no robot.

Mrs Wagstaff put her hand on the classroom door handle to go into the classroom – and got a nasty electric shock. She shrieked and ... woke up.

To her relief, she was still in her own bed. The clock on her bedside cabinet said six o'clock. What a terrible dream!

Then she realised she had no Class Z in her school. What was more, she had no badly-behaved children in St Griff's at all. Well, one or two, perhaps. Just like any other school, I suppose.

The message is

Children should not be afraid of their teachers but should always do their best to be well-behaved for them.

Share your thoughts with everyone

Is being a teacher a very hard job?

What do you think is the hardest part?

Think quietly about

Doing your best to make your teacher proud of you.

Songs to sing

Turn, turn, turn — *Alleluya* 32
I may speak — *Come & Praise* 100
Simple gifts — *Every Colour* 39
Can you hear? — *Harlequin* 33
I belong to a family — *Sing it in the Morning* 3
Mysteries — *Tinderbox* 40

Prayers

Page 221

PART II
SPECIAL DAYS

FESTIVALS AND CELEBRATIONS TRADITIONAL TO THE BRITISH ISLES

69 Traditional New Year

January

Theme

New Year Resolutions.

Background

Schools are closed over the New Year but, early in the spring term, teachers may find it interesting for children to compare notes about their individual experiences, especially if the old tradition of 'Resolutions' comes up.

Let's talk

When is New Year's Day?

When is New Year's Eve?

Tell us about anything special that you do on New Year's Eve.

What is a New Year Resolution?

Time to listen
If you make a New Year Resolution you should do your best to keep it.

Joe and a New Year Resolution

Joe's Grandad Ben used to be a sailor. One New Year's Eve, Joe took Grandad his usual New Year present from the family, an annual book called *Tales of the Sea*.

Grandad Ben was pleased with the new book and said, 'That makes twenty-three annuals I have now. Come and see where I keep them all.' They went upstairs, he opened the loft, climbed up the ladder and switched on the light in the loft.

'Come on up,' he said. The loft was piled high from floor to ceiling – books, stuffed animals, flags, and … oh, you name it, it was there.

'Grandad,' said Joe, 'There is so much stuff in here the floor is going to give way soon. Why do you keep it?'

The old man laughed and said, 'I hate throwing things away. Still, I will make a New Year Resolution to get rid of all of it. Except these books, of course.'

Joe scolded, 'You made a New Year Resolution last year. And the year before. Mum says you make the same promise every year. But you never keep it. It's no use making a New Year Resolution unless you do.'

'Well, I will this year,' chortled Grandad.

They went downstairs, they wished each other Happy New Year and Joe went out, slamming the front door, because it always stuck a bit. He was at the end of the path when there was a loud rumbling noise and he saw Grandad Ben rush out of the house.

Then the thatched roof of the cottage fell inwards, as if it was going down a giant plug-hole, and the four walls collapsed with a crash. A huge cloud of dust rose into the air. When it it had settled, all that was left was a big pile of rubble. The loft floor *had* given way, just as Joe had said it would. Grandad's pretty little cottage was now only a pile of bricks and timber.

Grandad shook the dust out of his thin hair and said, trying to smile, 'Well, at least I won't have to worry about keeping my New Year's Resolution now, will I? It's been kept for me!'

Joe did not know what to say. There wasn't a lot he could say, really, except 'I told you so', and nobody likes hearing that now, do they?

A pause for thought

Your house won't fall down if you don't keep a New Year Resolution but you might let yourself down.

Songs to sing

A New Year has started	*Sing a Song of Celebration* 25
Father Time	*Sing a Song of Celebration* 25
The miner's dream of home	*Okki-tokki-unga* 28
New things to do	*Tinderbox* 58

A poem for New Year

This kind of poem is called a *Haiku* and were first written in Japan. They have only three lines. Sometimes they rhyme but not very often.

Old and New

Ah, Old Year is dead,
Say Goodbye to him! Goodbye!
For New Year is born.'

Prayers

Page 221

70 Shrove Tuesday (Pancake Day) *February/March*

Theme

Making pancakes.

Background

The name 'Shrove Tuesday' comes from the expression 'to be shriven', the old name for confessing your sins on the last day before Lent.

The forty days of Lent are intended to be days of fasting to commemorate the time spent in the wilderness by Jesus Christ. Many Christians who observe Lent nowadays tend to give up one or more favoured luxuries instead of actually fasting, as their individual observance.

When Lent was strictly observed, people ate up all their best and tastiest food on Shrove Tuesday, often in the form of a large pancake filled with all kinds of foods. Non-Christian children may, of course, be familiar with Pancake Day, regardless of its Christian significance, purely from contact with other children, so there should be no risk of religious offence in using this assembly, provided religous connotations are not implied.

Let's talk

Who has pancakes at home on Pancake Day?

How are they cooked?

Tell me another name for Pancake Day.

Time to listen

Prudence Piglet tried tossing pancakes last year and she made a terrible mess. Some piglets never learn …

Heavy Pancakes

It was Pancake Day and Prudence decided to surprise her Mum with a lovely pile of golden pancakes when she came home from shopping. Sensibly, Prudence decided against tossing the pancakes because only expert cooks could do that. She would just turn the pancakes over in the pan, so as to cook on both sides, with a kitchen tool called a spatula.

Prudence found eggs and milk, but where was the flour? Then she spotted a plastic bag of white powder in the cupboard under the sink.

'Aha! Flour!' she cried and tipped it into a mixing bowl, along with the eggs and the milk and a pinch of salt. The little piglet stirred away at the mixture, singing her pancake song:

'Stir away, stir away,
Little pigs, it's Pancake Day,
Mix the pancakes, one, two, three,'
Yummy pancakes, wait and see!'

Then she poured half the mixture into the pan where it sizzled happily as Prudence carried on singing merrily:

'Lots of treacle, sugar too,
Golden-brown for me and you!'

But when she sniffed the sizzling batter in the pan, she stopped singing. It smelt most peculiar. Most peculiar indeed.

'Hm,' said the piglet, 'I'd better turn it over,' and she tried to push the spatula under the pancake to turn it over.

The pancake would not move. Prudence pushed again. but the spatula still would not shift the pancake. She shook the pan. She turned the pan upside down. Nothing happened. She banged the pan on the cooker, on the floor, on the table, on the doorstep and on her head (which hurt). The pancake stayed where it was.

Prudence began to panic. It was Mum's best frying-pan. She tried to hack the pancake off the pan with a carving knife from the drawer, which was rather silly of her. Nothing happened. The pancake was as solid as a rock.

The desperate piglet rushed out to the garden shed and grabbed one of Dad's hammers and bashed away at the pancake, but it did not even dent it. She banged and banged and banged – then the pancake and the bottom of the frying-pan fell out and landed on her trotter.

Prudence danced around the kitchen on one leg while nursing the other, snorting with pain as tears running down her snout. Perhaps it was just as well that Mrs Scratchings walked into the kitchen, just as her daughter fell on to the floor.

I won't tell you exactly what she said and did then because it might make *your* eyes water.

But I will tell you what Prudence had done wrong. The white powder she had used was not flour – it was the stuff that is mixed with water to fill holes in walls and in wood and it is very, very hard. Especially if it is fried.

Do I need to tell you that Prudence never tried making pancakes again?

A pause for thought

Piglets and people should never try cooking unless they know something about it.

A Poem for Pancake Day

This is not a serious poem – it might have been written by Prudence...

Pancakes

Take care when mixing your pancakes,
Be sure the mixture is right
Then cook them until they are golden,
Oh, I could eat pancakes all night!

But take care if you toss up your pancake,
Don't throw it too high in the air;
Because it might stick to the ceiling
Or fall down on grandfather's chair!

Songs to sing

Shrove Tuesday	*Harlequin* 9
Mix a pancake	*Harlequin* 10
Take the pancake mixture	*Sing a Song of Celebration* 29
Just a squeeze of lemon	*Sing a Song of Celebration* 29

Prayers

Page 222

71 St David's Day

1 March

Theme

The patron saint of Wales.

Background

Legend says that David was the grandson of King Ceredig of Wales, a cousin of King Arthur and a great miracle worker. He was born in the 6th century and became bishop of Menevia, now St David's. As head of the church in Wales he is believed to have founded many churches in the country. He died about 60 AD and was made a saint in 1120 AD.

Let's talk

(For those who live outside Wales)
Who can tell me how to travel to Wales from here?

What language do most Welsh people speak?

Is there a Welsh language?

Tell me anything you know about Wales.

Time to listen

A Welsh Story

Teacher: Some Welsh names are difficult for non-Welsh people to pronounce. It is less tiresome if assembly leaders attempt their own versions, hoping there are no Welsh-speaking children(or teachers) amongst the listeners. If you think they might criticise your efforts, suggest they might like to read the story …

This story may or may not be true, but then it is a very old story!

The Legend of Gelert, The Brave Dog

Long, long ago, Wales was a country ruled by a man who is famous to Welsh people, Prince Llewellyn. His home was in The Vale of Gwyant in North Wales, and he dearly loved his baby son, whose name, so I have been told, was Owain. The prince had a favourite hunting hound, Gelert, a brave and fearless dog.

One day, the prince was going on a hunting trip and the child's mother was away, visiting her sick father. She had not wished to take the child into a place of illness so Owain was left in Llewellyn's charge.

He could not imagine any danger inside the castle walls and told his baby's nurse to put the baby's crib in a small, sunny courtyard, with the trusty hound on guard.

Llewellyn returned early from his hunting – for some reason he had a feeling that something was wrong. Sure enough, when went into the courtyard, the baby's crib was nowhere to be seen.

Everyone rushed about, searching, but it was Llewellyn himself who came across a most dreadful sight. To his horror, he saw the faithful hound crouched near the crib, with blood dripping from its jaws! Mad with fury, and fearing the worst, Llewellyn drew up his sword and killed Gelert.

Then Llewellyn heard the baby crying. He rushed to the sound and saw his baby Owain, alive and well, and … the body of a huge wolf. It was obvious that Gelert had killed the wild animal, defending the baby Owain, and the blood was that of the wolf.

Llewelyn was terribly sorry for what he had done. All he could do was to bury the poor dog and build a memorial to his memory. A stone marking the spot is still to be seen in the valley and the place is now called Beddgelert or, in English, the grave of Gelert.

A pause for thought

This old Welsh story says that we should not to be in too much of a hurry to think that someone has done wrong.

Songs to sing

I have a tiny little house
(Welsh folk song) *Music Box Song Book* 86
David of the white rock *Musical Calendar of Festivals* 27
(This is quite a difficult song for KS1 children)
The bonny pit laddie *Music Box Song Book* 44
(At one time, there were many coal mines in Wales)
Click go the shears *Music Box Song Book* 17
(You will see many sheep on Welsh hillsides)

A Poem for St David's Day

St David's Day

The land returns from Winter
Like the saint from pilgrimage
Bringing with him a bird and a flower
Over mountains like dragons turned to stone.

Today repeats the yearly miracle
Along the valleys of the daffodil
And in the brightening sky above
St Davids's emblem is the dove.

Stanley Cook

Prayers

There are no special prayers for St David's Day.

*72 Mother's Day

March or April

Theme

Be thankful for Mothers.

Background

Mother's Day derives from the old church custom of attending the 'mother church' in their diocese. It became a time for honouring one's mother and for many years in the UK was known as Mothering Sunday. It disappeared in many parts of the country until 1942 when the American soldiers came here and reintroduced the celebration as Mother's Day. Since then, it has become very popular in the United Kingdom and has now assumed commercial importance.

Let's talk

Who can tell me about Mother's Day?

Time to listen

Ryan realises that some mothers are a lot better than others.

Nag, Nag, Nag

Edna Mortimer stood at the door of her son's bedroom and said sharply, 'Ryan, your room is a tip. Please tidy it up.'

Ryan looked up from his computer and groaned, 'What's wrong now? You're always moaning at me. Wash your face, clean your teeth, change your shirt and on and on and on. I wish I had a *normal* mother who doesn't nag, nag, nag all the time. I'm going out.' He stormed out, slamming the front door behind him.

Then something very strange happened to Ryan – he found himself in Broomstick Lane with no idea of how he got there. As he stood with his mouth open, he saw an old, bent woman who was carrying a basket of shopping.

She said in a trembly, old voice, 'You don't sound very happy, little boy. Have you got mother trouble?'

Ryan growled, 'I'm not a little boy, I'm ten years old and yes, I have got mother trouble. What of it?'

The old woman said, with a smile, 'Carry my shopping and I will cure the trouble for you.' Ryan followed the woman to a tumbledown old cottage. As he stood on the doorstep another strange thing happened – he found he was sitting in front of his computer again, as if nothing had happened!

But, over the next few days, he found that something *had* happened. His mother stopped nagging him, as he called it.

She never called him for meals and, when he did arrive, the food was cold and horrible. He got into trouble at school because Mother did not remind him to do his homework. His Mum did not remind him to shower, to change his clothes nor to clean his teeth. Soon after, he realised that his friends were holding their noses and saying, 'Pooh' whenever he went near them.

It was when Jordan, his best friend, told him that he smelt awful, that Ryan got the message.

He went home and told his Mum that he had been stupid and lazy and he was so sorry, so please could she be his Mum again, because all her grumbling was for his own good?

His mother said she had no idea what he was talking about and the more Ryan thought about it, he wondered if he had imagined everything that had happened. He wasn't even sure if anything *had* happened. It was all a bit of a mystery.

A pause for thought

If your mother grumbles at you it is usually for your own good.

Songs to sing

Mama don't 'low	*Tinderbox* 21
Supermum	*Tinderbox* 24
Mama lend me your pigeon	*Music Box Song Book* 62
She's the best Mum in the world	*Sing a Song of Celebration* 33
Only one mother for me	*Sing a Song of Celebration* 33

A Tanka Poem for Mother's Day

Tanka poems, like Haiku poems, were first written in Japan.

Each Tanka has 5 lines.

Try

Try on Mother's Day
To make your Mother happy;
Take her some flowers,
Chocolates would be lovely
But not as lovely as she.

Prayers

Page 222

73 St Patrick's Day

17 March

Theme

The patron saint of Ireland.

Background

Patrick was born in 387 AD, either in Wales or more probably near Dumbarton in Scotland. His father and grandfather were both Roman Christians. Patrick went to school but was not very interested in learning.

When he was 16, Irish raiders or pirates took him to Ireland and sold him as a slave to a chieftain in West Ireland. He became a shepherd, then he heard a voice in a dream which told him to travel on a ship. It is believed that he went to Tours in France and there became a bishop. He returned to Ireland as a missionary and possibly died in Saul, near Downpatrick, about 460 AD.

Let's talk

(For those who live outside Ireland)
How would you travel to Ireland from here?

What language do most Irish people speak?

Is there an Irish language?

Tell me anything else you know about Ireland.

Time to listen

In this old Irish story we are told that it is better to be polite than rude – especially to fairies!

Little Flaxy and a Hump

Once, in the little Irish village of Ballynonsuch, there lived a poor little man with a big hump on his back. Because he always wore a sprig of the blue flower in his old hat, the village people called him Flaxy.

One day, as Flaxy walked past the bubbly stream called the Feeny, he was sure he heard sweet voices singing a curious song:

'*Monday, Tuesday, Monday, Tuesday.*'

When the voices stopped Flaxy added in his jolly singing voice: 'Monday, Tuesday and what about Wednesday?' In a trice, Flaxy found himself being whisked down through the water by tiny, invisible hands to the bottom of the stream. There, dancing around him, he could see crowds of pretty little Irish fairies which are called leprechauns.

As they danced, the leprechauns sang a little verse:

'*To our song you've added more*
And now the hump that once you bore,
On your back shall be no more,
Look down now upon the floor.'

Flaxy found himself back on the bank where he looked down. Sure enough, there on the ground was his ugly hump. He rushed back to tell all the village folk and the news spread all round the county of Tipperick.

A week later a grumpy man called Sam Fladden, who had an even bigger hump than Flaxy, came to ask him if the leprechauns would do the same thing for him.

'Of course,' said Flaxy, 'The fairies of the Feeny stream sing a funny little song. All you do is add, "What about Wednesday?" just as I did.'

Sam Fladden did as he was told and, sure enough, he heard the fairies singing, '*Monday, Tuesday, Monday, Tuesday*'.

But instead of singing, 'And what about Wednesday?' he snarled, with his hands over his ears, 'Change the song, change the song, can't you? I'm sick of hearing the same thing over and over again!'

That made the fairies angry and they dragged Sam Fladden to the bottom of the river and sang:

'*Sam Fladden! Sam Fladden!*
Your voice came so bad in
The tune we felt glad in,
That your life we will sadden,
Take TWO humps, Sam Fladden!'

Then they whisked Sam Fladden back to the bank and there he stood with *two* humps on his back. And that is how he stayed for the rest of his life.

A pause for thought

It sounds like as if the leprechauns treated Sam Fladden very cruelly. Do you think he deserved it?

Songs to sing

Sing	*Every Colour* 50
St Patrick was a gentleman	*Musical Calendar of Festivals* 35
My Aunt Jane	*Musical Calendar of Festivals* 54

A Poem for St Patrick's Day

Old stories called legends tell us that St Patrick made all the snakes leave Ireland.

What snakes?

Old Ireland land of shamrock,
A country dressed in green,
St Patrick came long years ago,
Now no more snakes are seen.

Prayers

Page 223

74 Easter *March/April*

Theme

Easter eggs.

Background.

Easter eggs assume a great deal of importance to most children at Easter time. The custom holds no Christian significance and their origin has been linked with the celebration of the emergence of new life at spring time.

Children in Years R, 1 and 2 are not, by and large, very aware of the importance of Easter in the Christian calendar, except in denominational schools.

Let's talk

Tell me about any Easter eggs you hope to have.

Why do you think we have Easter eggs?

Time to listen

What happened to Millie has to be a dream, doesn't it?

A Magical Tree

'I'm sorry, Millie,' said Joe Peel, 'But we just can't afford to buy you any chocolate Easter eggs this year.'

Millie muttered, 'All my friends have chocolate eggs and it isn't fair.' She ran upstairs and flung herself on to her bed, still grumbling. Then she fell asleep.

She was woken by a tiny voice, squeaking, 'Millie! Will you come with me to Eggland?'

Sitting on the end of her bed was a blue rabbit wearing a bright blue coat and orange trousers. He whiffled his whiskers and Millie found herself on a hill of pink grass. All around, on peculiar trees, were the strangest, most brightly-coloured fruits she had ever seen.

'Try one,' said the blue rabbit, picking a brown, egg-shaped fruit. Millie bit into it – it was delicious chocolate filled with ice cream. It tasted so good so that she went to pick another one but the rabbit grabbed her hand.

'Come with me!' it giggled. Millie followed it to the top of the hill and gasped as she looked down at a little valley below.

Hundreds of little trees stood there, shaking their bright leaves and whispering, 'Hello, Millie, Hello Millie.'

But, best of all, every branch was gently shaking its fruit of Easter eggs, each one wrapped in coloured foil that glittered in the sunshine. Blue Rabbit gave her a gentle nudge. Down the hill she tumbled, roly-poly, coming to a stop under a pretty tree with gold-wrapped Easter eggs dangling from its branches.

Millie didn't wait to be asked. She grabbed the nearest egg, unwrapped it and gobbled the egg all up. Then another and another. And … surprise, surprise, she felt sick. Millie lay down and and fell asleep.

She woke to find herself looking at Hank, her one-eyed teddy bear who shared her pillow. She didn't feel sick any more, but, oh, she felt so disappointed. Still what a lovely dream!

Then she saw, in the early morning sunlight, as it streamed on to her quilt – a little piece of gold foil. Which smelt of … chocolate.

A pause for thought

Some children will not be able to eat chocolate Easter eggs.

Think of some reasons why not.

Songs to sing

My Easter bonnet	*Harlequin* 16
Hot Cross Buns	*Music Box Song Book* 55
	Musical Calendar of Festivals 36
This joyful Eastertide	*Musical Calendar of Festivals* 36
Pace Egging Song	*Musical Calendar of Festivals* 36
Hop along Easter bun	*Sing a Song of Celebration* 37
Sing out an Easter song	*Songs for Every Season* 51

A Poem about Easter Eggs

Did chocolate chicken
Lay this egg
Dressed silver, gold and rainbow,
Ribbon decked,
Sweets within?
And how
Did it get in the box?

Prayers

Page 222

75 St George's Day

23 April

Theme

The patron saint of England.

Background

Little is known about St George, who is also the patron saint of Portugal, but he may have been born in Turkey. Some say that he was killed in Nicodemia on 23 April, 303 AD. He was taken as England's patron saint in 1349 and is commemorated in several ways, such as the naming of St George's Chapel at Windsor Castle.

Let's talk

When is St George's Day?

What flag can you sometimes see on St George's Day?

Are there any other times when you see the English flag (eg at sporting events)?

Time to listen

Teacher: Two readings are offered.

The first is a narrative, rather than a story, and is more suitable for an assembly which aims to explain a little about the origins of the Saint's status. Although his origins are placed within the Christian tradition, the assembly is intended to be no more than an explanation of his supposed conquest of a dragon. The second is light-hearted fiction, apart from the fact that St George was almost certainly a real person.

Listening 1

England's Saint

It has been said that St George was born in the country called Turkey about 1700 years ago. He became a Roman soldier. In those days, the Emperor of Rome said that people who believed that Jesus Christ was God's Son should be killed.

The story says that St George thought this was wrong. He became a Christian himself and went home to Turkey where he had a suit of silver armour made, with a red cross painted on it, while his horse's harness was gold in colour.

He chose a cross because it is the sign of Christianity, and red because it is the colour of blood. The same thing was painted on his shield, too. The flag of St George, which we often see flying on English buildings on 23 April, is a white flag with a red cross on it.

When George was ready to spread the story of Jesus, he set off on his journeys. We do not know what happened to him afterwards, but some say that he was tortured and killed by the Romans for being a Christian.

One story says that he came to a city in North Africa called Silene, to be told that a fierce dragon was eating the sheep and cattle that belonged to the people. Then the dragon killed a shepherd boy, and ate him too, leaving only his bones. So the people decided to feed the dragon with two sheep a day, but they ran out of sheep. All they could think of then, was to leave children for the dragon to eat.

They had a lottery and, each day, a child was tied up and left for the dragon to eat. One day it was the turn of the king's daughter. George saw what was happening and he fought and killed the dragon. What happened afterwards in the story, no one knows. Perhaps George married the princess?

What we do know is that about 900 years ago George became Saint George and, later, he was chosen to be England's special saint. We call a special saint like this a *patron* saint. For example, St Crispin is the patron saint of travellers. As well as being the patron saint of two countries, St George is also patron saint of the Scouts, including, of course, Brownies and Rainbows, Cubs and Beavers.

Listening 2

In this story the dragon can think of better things to do than fighting.

The Dragon Wants to Read

Saint George Fitzdipp was not one of those people who are called 'saint' because they are ever such good people. It was just that when he was born, his mother fancied calling her son 'Saint'.

I am told that there was a real Saint George somewhere else, doing brave deeds, like fighting dragons, but I don't know about that. Anyway, one day, our Saint George rode into the village of Puffington so that his horse, Champion, could have a drink.

As Champion drank, George heard a woman bellowing fiercely, 'Oi. You. That's my horse trough and it's two pence a drink.' Saint George was too much of a gentleman to argue so he paid up, then introduced himself.

'I'm Mrs Tremble, Knight-person,' growled the woman, 'Are you any good at fighting dragons?' She was not to know that Saint George had never even seen a dragon, let alone fought one.

George mumbled, 'I haven't really had a lot of practice. Why?'

'Because there's one up on the Top Meadow, and it is time it left,' bawled Mrs Tremble. 'Get rid of it and I'll give you supper. How about it?'

Saint George decided that he would rather face a dragon than argue with Mrs Tremble, so he agreed. He found the dragon in the field easily enough, because it was lying down, holding an open reading-book and blowing puffs of smoke from its nostrils as it muttered, 'c-a-t says cat'.

The creature, which was no bigger than a Shetland pony, saw him and groaned, 'Oh, not another brave knight. Why can't you leave me alone to learn how to read? I can't stand all this fighting stuff.'

'A woman in the village said I was to – er- get rid of you,' said Saint George carefully.

'That stupid Tremble woman,' snapped the dragon, 'She says dragons make her itch. Never heard such nonsense.' Saint George stood there, not knowing what to do next.

Then he had an idea and said, brightly, 'I say! Tell you what! I'll teach you to read! Then you could do me a favour by *pretending* to go away.'

The dragon looked pleased and said, 'I like it. OK, it's a deal.' And so it was that Saint George not only taught a dragon to read but made a friend for life. But neither he nor the dragon told Mrs Tremble about their bargain. Well, would you?

A pause for thought

Saint George may not have fought a dragon but he was still a brave man who was not afraid to say out loud what he believed.

Songs to sing

Maggon, the bad-tempered dragon	*Apusskidu* 55
Song for Saint George	*Musical Calendar of Festivals* 43
Song for a bragging dragon	*Silly Aunt Sally* 52
Let's pretend	*Tinderbox* 25
Puff, the magic dragon	*Tinderbox* 50

A not-too-serious poem about St George and the Dragon

St George met a fearful dragon
Which was breathing out flames and green smoke,
And he said, 'Please stop eating the children,
Your diet's no longer a joke.
They fought hard with sword and with fire,
Then decided to call it a draw,
And they sat down to tea and hot crumpets
Which was much more relaxing than war!

Prayers

Page 223

76 May Day *1 May*

Theme

The celebration of May Day.

Background

At primary school level (Key Stages 1 and 2) we do not need to consider May Day as a political and industrial celebration, rather giving our attention to its significance as a ceremony related to ancient custom.

The origin of May Day is in Celtic lore and heralded the start of summer. The Maypole was possibly a fertility symbol, as was the dance described below.

Let's talk

Tell me about May Day and Maypoles.

(If no information is forthcoming, go straight into the narrative).

Time to listen

Teacher: Two readings are offered. The first narrative describes, briefly, a typical Maypole dance which is still to be seen in many communities, rural and urban, probably more performed by children rather than adults.

Listening 1

Maypole Dancing

At one time, the Maypole dance was done by women and not children. The Maypole was a tall pole, usually made from a tree trunk which had been trimmed and smoothed and probably painted in bright colours. Each woman danced a hopping, skipping step round the Maypole, whilst holding different coloured ribbons that were fastened to the top of the pole. The pole was often capped with a carved 'crown'.

Some of the dancers went in one direction and others danced the opposite way, changing direction now and again. As the dancers passed one another, some went on the outside of the circle and some went inside. This meant the ribbons became plaited.

As they wrapped tighter and tighter round the Maypole, the ribbons got shorter and the dancers had to dance nearer and nearer to the pole. Then they all went the opposite way to which they started and ended up as they had begun, with the ribbons long again.

Some people think that the short ribbons stood for the short days we have in winter. As spring comes, the days get longer. just as the ribbons do in the second half of the dance.

Listening 2

Emergency! Murdered Maypole!

The children of the school in Parsonsdown village had celebrated the first day of May – May Day – for years by putting up their school's Maypole and dancing round it.

The time had come round again, the children were all ready and all that had to be done was to fix new coloured ribbons to the Maypole.

The Head Teacher, Mrs Rose, went down into the cellar under the church, where the pole was stored, to check whether the Maypole needed a new coat of white paint. She turned on the light and – an army of mice ran away from the precious pole. To her dismay, she saw that the mice had gnawed away great chunks of it and the pole would be quite useless.

Sadly, she told the children what had happened. None of the suggestions they were made were any good until Mollie Poulter, one of the children in Year 6, said, 'Leave it to me, Mrs Rose, I'll sort it. Just give me the ribbons.'

Mrs Rose was very doubtful but Mollie was a very sensible girl, so she decided she had to trust her. There was nothing to lose, anyway. The morning of May Day, which was a school holiday, arrived. Mollie called at Mrs Rose's cottage and asked the Head Teacher to go with her to the village green.

Mrs Rose was delighted to see, shining in the May sunshine, a splendid, brand-new gleaming-white Maypole, with brightly coloured ribbons hanging from the gold crown at the top.

'That's wonderful, Mollie,' she cried, 'But however did you manage that?'

Mollie smiled a huge smile, 'My dad is a telephone engineer for British Telecom, isn't he?'

So can you tell me what the Maypole was made from?

A pause for thought

Children can often surprise grown-ups with their good ideas.

Songs to sing

It happens each spring	*Harlequin* 15
Tomorrow is the first of May	*Musical Calendar of Festivals* 45
May garlands	*Musical Calendar of Festivals* 45
All the flowers are waking	*Someone's Singing, Lord* 48

A Poem for May Day

Maypole

In and out weave, ribbons
Around the Maypole.
Turn, twist, flow
Around the Maypole.
Tip and toe
Around the Maypole.
Shape the pattern Flow, twist, turn
Around the Maypole
To dress her
All in finery.

Prayers

Page 222

*77 Fathers' Day *June*

Theme

Thinking about fathers.
[*Teacher*: This could be a highly sensitive subject]

Time to listen

Father doesn't always know best but he does sometimes.

Herbert Goes Fishing

'Dad,' said Herbert Hopskip, 'Can I go fishing up at Pike Pool?'

Hannibal Hopskip put down his newspaper, wiggled his whiskers and said, with a frown, 'No you can't. It's not safe.'

'Why not?' whined Herbert. 'I can look after myself.'

His dad replied, sharply, 'Young man, children do *not* argue with their fathers. Just take my word for it that Pike Pool is not a safe place for little rabbits. Now go out to play.' But instead Herbert sneaked into the garden shed, grabbed his fishing rod and a pot of maggots and headed for Pike Pool.

In no time at all, he had cast his hook into the water and sat on the bank to enjoy himself. He was just nodding off to sleep in the hot sun when he saw that his float was bobbing up and down – a bite! Herbert yanked away at his rod. Out came the hook, but there was no maggot on it. There was no fish, either.

'This won't do,' grumbled Herbert and he leaned over to look into the water, still holding his rod.

Then he got the shock of his life. A *gigantic* pike, the biggest fish he had ever seen, leapt out of the water and grabbed his long, left ear in its huge, sharp teeth. Herbert screamed and lashed out at the monster with his fishing rod. It let his ear go and the little rabbit fell back on to the bank, panting with fright. His ear hurt but it did not bleed, so he ran all the way home.

Later, he told his father what had happened. Dad did not tell Herbert off. He did tell him that he had been attacked by the most feared fish in the whole of Nibbletown and he was lucky to have got away with only losing half an ear.

Herbert rushed to look in the mirror. When he saw himself he screeched with horror. Half of his left ear had gone!

And ever since then, Herbert has been known as Herbert Half-ear Hopskip. He is also known as the rabbit who *always* listens to his father. Mind you, I do think that Mr Hopskip might have told Herbert *why* Pike Pond was so dangerous. What do you think?

A pause for thought

Father's advice may be worth remembering on Father's Day.

Songs to sing

A still, small voice	*Come & Praise* 96
Johnny get your hair combed	*Music Box Song Book* 13
Hush, little baby	*Musical Calendar of Festivals* 59
I belong to a family	*Sing it in the Morning* 3
Consider yourself at home	*Sing a Silver Lining* 16

A Poem for Father's Day

My Dad Said

Today is the feast day
of Saint Settee
And on the feast day
of Saint Settee
we must all be quiet
on the settee
We must not play football
on the settee
We must not draw with felt tips
on the settee
We must not lose our crisps
down the settee
We must not push the dog
under the settee
We must not jump screaming
over the settee
For the wrath of Saint Settee
is a terrible thing
My dad said.

Martyn Wiley and Ian McMillan

Prayers

Page 222

78 Harvest Festival

Theme

Be thankful for Harvest.

Background

Although harvest time is less significant than it used to be, because we are no longer totally dependent on our own seasonal crops, we should still be grateful that few people in this country go short of food, from whatever source. At the same time children should appreciate that farmers are relieved when their harvest is home because of the vagaries of our weather.

Let's talk

Not all harvest is corn and fruit. Tell me about some other kinds of harvest.

Time to listen

Horace Harvest Mouse saves the day!

Mouse-teeth and a Tractor

'Oh, we are lucky to have this comfortable little nest here on this wheatstalk,' sighed Hilda Harvest Mouse contentedly.

'Indeed we are,' agreed her husband Homer, sleepily.

Then his youngest son Harvey rushed into the nest, sqeaking excitedly, 'Dad, Dad! Farmer Turnup is fixing the reaper on to his tractor to cut his corn!'

Homer leapt up from his comfy mouse-chair, and gasped, 'He is early this year! There won't be time to move everything to the nest I have built in the winter-wheat field!'

Horace, the eldest son, looked up from his mouse-book and said, with a grin, 'OK, Dad, don't worry. Filbert Fieldmouse knew this would happen. He showed told me how to spoil the farmer's plans. For a short while, anyway.'

Hilda Harvest Mouse lifted her paws in dismay. 'Oo, my dear boy, you won't do anything dangerous, will you?'

'Stay mouse-cool, Ma,' laughed Horace, 'Trust us. We'll fix the tractor.' And off he and Harvey scuttled in the direction of the farmer's barn. I don't know what the cheeky little mice did, but, an hour later, Farmer Turnup was still trying to start his tractor.

The harvest mice knew he was having trouble because they could hear him making *very* bad-tempered noises. Eventually, he gave up and went indoors to call the garage, because he knew nothing at all about tractor engines. The engineer arrived next morning, by which time the harvest mice had moved to their new house.

I don't know any more about tractors than Farmer Turnup does but I do know that Horace and Harvey had nibbled some electric wires in the engine with their sharp little teeth.

It was a shame about the farmer's plans, I suppose, but he did get all his wheat cut the following day. So the little mice didn't do too much harm after all.

A pause for thought

The harvest is important to all kinds of life – for different reasons.

Songs to sing

Now we sing a harvest song	*Come & Praise* 138
Harvest, harvest, come along	*Every Colour* 3
Oats and beans	*Music Box Song Book* 14
The cockle gatherer	*Music Box Song Book* 18
Watch the combine harvester go	*Sing a Song of Celebration* 7
See the golden fields of corn	*Sing a Song of Celebration* 7
Look for signs that summer's done	*Sing it in the Morning* 19

A Poem for Harvest Time

Whispering wheat dozes
Ripe and fat,
Across from the houses of hay;
While the snorting red monster
Creaks, groans, roars,
Belching blue breath,
Across from the houses of hay;
Rumbles towards its gathering
Of the sleepy goldness
That makes our daily bread.

Prayers

Page 222

*79 Hallowe'en *31 October*

Theme

Warning younger children about 'Trick or Treat'.

Background

Hallowe'en was originally a Scottish name for the Christian vigil on the eve of All Hallows or All Saints Day. Over the years it became linked with witchcraft and its practices. For that reason, it has not, lately, been celebrated in the majority of schools.

The import of 'Trick and Treat' from the USA, however, has revived interest in the day as one of 'Ghoulies and Ghosties and 'Things that go bump in the night' and many families now hold Hallowe'en parties. It is, however, 'Trick and Treat' a practice, which can disturb nervous or elderly people if it becomes at all threatening, which is the subject of this assembly.

The assembly is designed for Year 2, but could be used beyond Key Stage 1, if considered appropriate.

Let's talk

Tell me if you do 'Trick and Treat'.

Is it safe the way you do it – for you?

Has it ever worried the people to whom you do it? Perhaps you don't know.

Time to listen

Lottie Turns the Tables

'I thought so,' said Lottie Binkle, looking at her calendar, 'October 31st tomorrow. Hallowe'en. Trick or Treat. Those kids frightened me to death last year. But not this time.'

Next day, Lottie was very busy with needle and iron as she hummed a little tune to herself. After tea, at six o'clock, Lottie sat down to wait for the visitors. Sure enough, there came a rat-a-tat-tat on the front door of Rose Cottage. She went to the front door and peeped through her spy-hole.

In the moonlight she could see four sniggering children, aged about nine, two boys and two girls, wearing masks – a gorilla, an alien, a vampire and a dinosaur.

'Go on, then, Troy,' hissed Daisy Warble to the biggest boy. 'Knock on the door.'

He gave her a shove and growled, 'Gerroff. I'm going to. Is everybody ready?' Everybody nodded, he grabbed hold of the gleaming brass knocker and banged hard. To his surprise, the door opened at once, just a little way.

An old, cracked voice said, 'Yes? What do you want?'

The four children all chanted, 'Trick or Treat, Trick or Treat, we'll scare you stiff if we don't eat!'

The door was flung open wide and they saw a sight which would keep them awake that night and a few more besides. Framed in an eerie red light, they saw a hideous, green-faced old crone, with a tall, pointed hat, waving a glowing green stick above her head.

'*You* will scare *me* stiff, will you, eh? she cackled, 'Ha ha ha ha ha! I think not. Because I am now about to change you all into … slugs and snails!'

She raised the glowing stick and chanted, 'Trick and Treat, Trick and Treat, This old witch you cannot beat. …'

But the Trickers and Treaters had gone, running up the lane faster than they had ever run before. Lottie watched them disappear into the dark, as she leaned against the door-post, laughing so much that she felt weak.

She took off her hat and her witch costume which she had last worn in a play thirty years before, and went to make some cocoa.

As she sat down in her comfy armchair to drink it, she said, still laughing, 'I enjoyed that. The best Trick and Treat I ever had. And it was all mine!'

A pause for thought

Make certain that grown-ups allow you to do 'Trick or Treat' before you go!

You may not be scared by your game, because there are no such things as real live witches nor old ladies who who dress up in 'witchy' clothes to frighten children, like the one in the story. Just remember that some of the people you call on may not enjoy it as much as you do, so don't knock on the doors of strangers or people who aren't expecting you. And, whatever you do, don't be *rude*!

Songs to sing

There was an old witch
Things that go bump in the night
Halloween's coming
Jack O'Lantern
Hallowe'en Calypso
Hallowe'en is coming

Apusskidu 17
Flying around 53
Harlequin 35
Musical Calendar of Festivals 90
Silly Aunt Sally 10
Tinderbox 61

Trick or Treat Tanka

Knock soft on the door
And hope it is not dark den
Of witch or wizard,
Because, young Tricker, Treater,
You may not enjoy the Treat!

Prayers

Page 223

80 Woosh and crackle

5 November

Theme

Reminders about safety on Bonfire Night.

Let's talk

When is Bonfire Night?

What is another name for Bonfire Night (looking for 'Guy Fawkes')?

Why is it called 'Guy Fawkes' Night (briefly!)?

Tell me about your plans for Bonfire Night.

Time to listen

Charlie and Beth could hardly believe their ears – well, would you?

Or Would You Rather be a Guy?

'What if it rains and puts out the bonfire and I won't burn on November 5th?' said the strange, creepy voice from the top of the bonfire.

Charlie and Beth both heard it at the same time.

Charlie, with his hair standing on end, croaked, 'Am I going dotty or did I hear someone say something?' His sister's teeth were chattering so much that she could only nod. The children looked nervously up at the guy sitting in the old armchair on the top of the big bonfire. Cheerily, it waved the old umbrella tied to its hand and grinned at them with its friendly, painted smile.

'You heard me, this is your guy talking,' said the guy, 'And the bonfire and I are awfully wet. Still, it might save a few accidents if the bonfire *won't* burn.' Suddenly, Beth was not scared any more.

'What do you mean, Mr Guy?' she said, boldly, 'What accidents?'

The guy took off its battered hat, scratched its straw head and replied, 'Oh, you know, like last year when Micky Muggins threw a firework in the bonfire and got a nasty burn when the firework blew up in his face. And Freda Fudge who lit a banger and threw it at Billy Blipp on the other side.

And Sonia Stoodle whose banger went off in her hand. They were all in hospital for weeks.'

'Oh, *those* accidents,' said Charlie, rather rudely, 'It was their own silly faults. Stupid kids.'

The guy replaced its hat and said in its gruff voice, 'Yes, accidents like that. But that was *last* year. Will the same things happen again this year? Do you two know about things you are supposed to do and things you are supposed not to do when there are bonfires and fireworks about?'

Charlie and Beth tried to speak together, 'Oh, yes … we … must … keep … pets … don't …'

'You *are* keen!' laughed the guy, 'One at a time, please. You first, girl. Tell me three things to do to be safe.'

Beth screwed up her face and said, 'One: Always keep a firework in a box until it is time to let it off. Two: Get a grown-up to light the firework. Three: Keep well back from fireworks that are going off and keep away from the bonfire.'

The guy clapped its straw hands in their battered old gloves and chortled, 'Good, Good! Now, boy, tell me some things you must not do.'

Charlie, feeling very confident, said, counting on his fingers, 'One: Never go close to a firework which has not gone off. Two: Never try to relight a firework that has gone out. Three: Never throw fireworks, *anywhere*, especially into the bonfire. Four: Never put fireworks in your pocket. Five: Never put fireworks into bottles, not even rockets.'

'Splendid, splendid,' the guy guffawed, 'I think you both know the rights and wrongs of fireworks. Well done! But isn't there one more thing people should do on Bonfire Night?'

'Oh, yes cried, 'Beth, 'We should keep all our pets indoors so they won't be scared. Isn't that right, guy?' But there was no reply – the guy just sat there, a friendly, painted smile on its face. which was made from an old sheet …

He might have winked but Beth and Charlie were not at all certain about that. But they were certain that they would remember all the things they had told the guy. And I hope you will do the same.

A pause for thought

Whatever you think of talking guys, on Bonfire Night, follow the Fireworks Code.

Songs to sing

The Fireman	*Apusskidu* 33
Round, round, round	*Come & Praise* 111
The fifth of November	*Harlequin* 38
Guy Fawkes	*Musical Calendar of Festivals* 96
November 5th	*Sing a Silver Lining* 12
Let us remember	*Sing a Silver Lining* 12

Five Haiku about Bonfire and Fireworks

Bonfire, crackle, spit,
Rocket fizz, zoom, blossom, die,
Golden sparklers dance.

Catherine Wheel turn,
Roman candle hiss, explode.
Banger thunder clap!

Jumping Jack hop, skip,
Golden rain showers watchers,
Look, the guy burns bright!

Sparks flutter through smoke
Stoke up the sagging bonfire
Warm cold hands on blaze.

The fire collapses now,
Nervous children move well away
And soon the night will win.

Prayers

Page 223

81 Poppies and parades

November

Theme

Remembrance Day – what's going on?

Let's talk

Sunday is Remembrance Day and poppies are being sold (in school/on the streets/from door-to-door).

Tell me anything you can about Remembrance Day.

Who knows anyone who was in a war?

Was everybody brave when there was a war?

Do people have to be in a war to be brave?

When might ordinary people show how brave they can be?

Time to listen

This story tells us about a man who was not in a war, but wanted others to *think* he was brave, even though he was not. He was so keen that he told lies to make them think that he was brave.

The Man who Wanted to be Brave

Long, long ago in Australia, before white men arrived in their big ships, there lived a very timid man called Hakona.

He often pretended, when he was alone, that he was fighting the fierce, one-eyed creatures called Ozzieweems that lived in the outback, the Australian desert.

Of course, he would beat them every time.

One day, he stabbed away at the air, with his stone-headed spear, pretending that he was fighting Ozzieweems. But all he killed was … ten flies!

'Well, they might have been Ozzieweems,' said Hakona and he carved these words on to the spear: 'With this spear of stone, Hakona killed ten Ozzieweems.'

One moon later, he decided to go walkabout in the outback. It was so hot that he fell asleep in the shade of a eucalyptus tree. As he slept, along came seven four-eyed Jumbuckies, deadly enemies of the Ozzieweems, riding on kangaroos. They read what it said upon Hakona's spear.

'Oho!' cried one, 'This little two-eyed creature looks like a great warrior. He has already killed ten of our enemies! 'Let us make him chief of our tribe.'

All the others agreed and when Hakona woke up they asked him to be their chief. Hakona said he would try it for a while.

Next day, one hundred Ozzieweems arrived, looking for a fight. The Jumbuckies asked their new chief to lead them into battle.

Hakona was terrified at the idea, but chose a quiet-looking kangaroo to ride and hoped for the best. Now riding a kangaroo is not easy and the animal bolted, with Hakona hanging on round its neck as it it bounced along – boi-ing boi-ing boi-ing! He grabbed hold of a wally-tree and pulled it up from the sand, roots and all and the kangaroo bolted towards the Ozzieweem army. The tree that Hakona carried kicked up so much dust that the one-eyed Ozzieweems could not see and thought they were being attacked by hundreds of Jumbuckies.

They ran away, howling, back to their own land. The Jumbuckies said that Hakona was the bravest warrior in the world. I am sorry to tell you, that Hakona thought so, too. But you and I know better, don't we?

A pause for thought

It takes real courage to be brave when you are really very frightened.

Songs to sing

A better world	*Alleluya* 60
Kangaroos like to hop	*Music Box Song Book* 69
Tell me	*Sing it in the Morning* 24
There's something about a soldier	*Ta-ra-ra-boom-de-ay* 46
Let it be	*Tinderbox* 48

A Cinquain Poem for Remembrance Day

A Cinquain is is a kind of English Haiku or Tanka and has a pattern of its own.

Red Poppies

Poppies
Glow red through grey,
Of chill November day
And medals on old proud soldiers
Shine bright.

Prayers

There are no special prayers for Remembrance Day.

82 St Andrew's Day

30 November

Theme

The patron saint of Scotland.

Background

Andrew is the only patron saint of the United Kingdom who is said to have been present during the ministry of Jesus Christ.

He was a fisherman at the village of Bethsaida in Palestine and became an important person in Christianity, until he was killed by the Romans for being a Christian. He was crucified on a cross shaped like a letter X, in AD 70. A cross shaped like this is now known as a St Andrew's Cross and a white one can be seen on the blue Scottish flag.

Let's talk

(For those who live outside Scotland)

Who can tell me how to travel to Scotland from here?

What language do most Scottish people speak?

Is it different from the English that we speak?

Is there a Scottish language?

Note: Evidently, Scottish schools using this book will have to consider how this assembly is approached. The basic historical facts of the story are accurate, although like the Scottish legend, some parts of the story can only be imaginary.

Time to listen

This story is not so much about a famous Scotsman as a lesson he learned when he thought everything had gone wrong.

Robert Bruce and the Spider

Robert Bruce, King of Scotland, had never felt less like a king as he flung open the door of the empty cottage and collapsed face down on to the bed of dirty straw.

He was on the run again, after yet another terrible defeat of his brave Scottish warriors. by the power of the English army in this year 1314. It seemed to him that soon King Edward II would rule Robert Bruce's beloved land for ever.

'My bravehearts can take no more,' he groaned, 'Soon there will be none left but old men and boys to fight the invader.' He turned over on to his back and made up his mind that he would not be King of Scotland for much longer.

'What's the use?' he said, miserably, 'Scotland is lost and I can fight no more. What is the point of trying?'

Then something caught his eye. A fat spider, busy up in the beams of the tumbledown cottage, was hanging from its web and trying to swing itself from one beam to another.

Fascinated, Robert watched the little creature swinging. On its first swing it fell short of its target. But it did not give up. It tried again, once, twice, three times... five times more!

Robert Bruce sat up, clenched his fists and said to the spider, 'If you try again and reach the beam on your seventh attempt then I will try again to resist the armies of the English King Edward.' The spider did not answer, but swung again. This time – success! It reached the beam.

Robert Bruce was as good as his word. The spider had taught him that one should not give up too easily, but to try again until all hope has gone. Having learned this lesson, he rallied all the Scots who could still fight and, because they believed in him, they won battle after battle. Then came the last battle of all, the Battle of Bannockburn. The English were defeated and ran away. Robert was truly King of Scotland and reigned for 24 years.

But he never forgot that little spider and the lesson it had taught him.

A pause for thought

Everybody, king or no, can learn from the smallest creatures.

Songs to sing

You can do it	*Sing a Silver Lining* 9
Say, bonnie lassie	*Music Box Song Book* 61
I can climb	*Every Colour* 17
Somebody greater	*Come & Praise* 5
Try again	*Tinderbox* 58
New things to do	*Tinderbox* 65

A Not-too-serious poem about a well-known Scottish dish

Background

Haggis is a traditional Scottish dish, although of French origin. It is made from sheep offal, herbs and condiments and mixed with oatmeal. The mixture is boiled for three hours in a haggis bag. This is, traditionally, a sheep's stomach, but those who prepare haggis nowadays may well use an alternative bag. Again, traditionally, it is served on Burns Night (January 25th) and is brought into the dining room to the music of the bagpipes. Non-Scots often view the haggis with some suspicion …

The Mysterious Haggis

The haggis is a wawlie beast
Aye, on it Scots folk like to feast,
It has nae hair, it has nae tail,
And, oh! Its skin is unco pale!
The haggis is of mighty fame
It is nae wild but tasty tame
Wi' wondrous filling is stuffed tight
And bagpipes skirl for auld Burns' Night.

**According to Robert Burns:*
wawlie = fat/plump; Aye = yes; nae = no/not; wi' = with
unco = very; skirl = The sound of the bagpipes; auld = old

Prayers

Page 223

83 Christmas time *December*

Theme

Father Christmas or Santa Claus.

Let's talk

Tell me what you know about Father Christmas.

Time to listen

This story is about a modern way to get in touch with Father Christmas.

Website www.FatherChristmas.Farnorth

At six o'clock on one dark, cold Christmas morning, Edward Holliberry sat up in bed, his teeth chattering with cold and excitement. The time was six o'clock.

'Father Christmas must have have been,' he said excitedly, 'I'm sure I heard his sleigh bells last night.' He grabbed the long, black stocking off the bedpost where he had hung it the night before. But, to his dismay, the stocking was empty. No toys. No oranges. No chocolate. Not even a pink sugar mouse. There was no doubt – jolly Father Christmas had *not* called at 17 Fishbone Street, Toggleham. And there were no exciting parcels on his bed, either.

Edward rushed into his parents' bedroom and jumped on the bed, yelling and sobbing all at the same time, 'Mum! Dad! Mum! Dad! Father Christmas hasn't been. He hasn't left me any prezzies! Why, Mum? Why, Dad? I've not been naughty, have I?'

Edward bawled for the rest of the morning until his Uncle Rudolf, who had a *very* red nose, arrived for dinner. His uncle gave him a present of a remote-control car which made the little boy feel a bit better. After dinner, Uncle Rudolf disappeared into the den where Mungo's dad kept his computer. When he came back, he was smiling all over his face and his nose was even more rosy than usual.

'I've sent an e-mail letter on the Internet, to Father Christmas,' announced Uncle Rudolf, 'At: www dot Fatherchristmas dot farnorth. Now we must wait and see what happens. Just make sure you hang up your stocking tonight.'

Nothing happened for the rest of the day, although Edward ate far too much turkey and pudding but, the next morning, when he woke up ...! On his bed was a *huge* pile of presents, his stocking was full of toys and sweets and, pinned on his door, was a letter, written in beautiful handwriting. It said:

'Dear Edward,

I am so sorry to have missed you, but my elves got mixed up with another Edward Holliberry. I didn't think there could be two people with a name like yours, so you must excuse me, especially as he lives at 17, Fishtail Road, Tinkleham. So he has all your toys and stuff but I don't think he will be very interested because he is 93 years old.

I have left you some extra presents to make up for my mistake.

Happy Boxing Day!

Love from

Father Christmas xxx'

And that was the very best Boxing Day that Edward was ever to have in the whole of his life.

A pause for thought

Think about all those children who do not know what a happy time Christmas can be.

Songs to sing

Happy Christmas	*Flying a Round* 66
Pull the cracker – BANG!	*Harlequin* 40
Last night as I lay sleeping	*Music Box Song Book* 116
Santapiece	*Silly Aunt Sally* 2
The Nativity Song	*Sing a Song of Celebration* 19
Go tell it on the mountain	*Sing it in the Morning* 8

and: Any songs from *Merrily to Bethlehem* or *Carol, Gaily Carol*

A Christmas Poem

Christmas Eve Night

Christmas is when you wake before the light,
Mole up the stockings to find what might
Be there in stocking or on bed.
Has Father Christmas been
Or someone in his stead?
Fingers recognize the orange and the nuts,
A book is well easy to the touch,
But what is this? Its shape will not betray
Its secret, that must wait till day.
So meanwhile, snuggle up,
Pull up the sheets
And wait for the dawn
With its Christmas Day treats.

John Cotton

Prayers

Page 223

PART III
SPECIAL DAYS

FESTIVALS AND CELEBRATIONS ORIGINATING IN CULTURES NOT NATIVE TO THE BRITISH ISLES

These assemblies are suggested to mark special days as celebrated by other cultures.

No teaching or discussion on any aspect of the religious faiths is involved. Nor do the stories owe their origins to any dogma or legend of the ethnic faith commemorated, apart from taking one of the major tenets or aspects of a faith, where applicable, as a theme.

A brief background is given to each celebration but, unless the assembly leader considers it appropriate for the age group, the assembly should be conducted at face value, as it were – a celebration from a non-British culture from which everyone can learn and benefit

The stories can be read at the time of any other celebration of a particular faith if wished or whenever the stories seem appropriate, regardless of any connection with the points of origin.

84 At the time of a Japanese Festival: New Year (Shinto religion)

January

Background

Most religious Japanese people follow either the ancient Shinto religion, Buddhism or Confucianism. Shintoism is an ancient religion of Japan. Its beginnings were founded in the worship of nature, then of many gods. The veneration of heroes came later, culminating in devotion to the person of the Emperor, who was worshipped as a descendant of the sun goddess, Amaterasu. Japan now uses the Western Gregorian calendar and Japanese families who follow the Shinto tradition prepare for New Year by cleaning their houses on 13 December. They decorate houses as New Year's Day approaches and exchange gifts on New Year's Day itself. It is a time for forgiveness of those who have done harm or given offence. A traditional meal of vegetable stew with rice cakes and other vegetables is eaten.

A considerable number of Japanese nationals now live in the United Kingdom and some schools might find they are able to invite guests into school to talk about their culture and religions.

Let's talk

Where is Japan?

What language do they speak?

Do you have anything in your house made in Japan (TV, computer, radio, VCR, DVD etc)?

Tell us the name of a Japanese car.

* *If there are no Japanese children in the school:*

Who knows any Japanese people? Tell us about them.

Who knows anything about Japanese food?

Who knows anything else about Japan?

Time to listen

The Farmer, the Fox and the Fireworks: a Japanese Story

Farmer Kantana Noguchi, who lived near the village of Noda, was very proud of his chickens, because each fine brown bird laid a delicious brown egg every day.

One dark night he heard his chickens squawking, and rushed out to their coop, but he could see nothing because it was so dark. Next morning, he opened the door to wish his chickens 'Ohayo' (which is the Japanese way of saying 'Good morning') because, in those days, Japanese farmers always treated their chickens with great respect. To his dismay, two chickens were missing. All that was left of them were two piles of feathers.

'O! My chickens-chan!' (which is the Japanese way of saying, 'O! My dear chickens!'), 'Who has taken you and left nothing but feathers?'

Then, to his surprise, he heard Chicken Mariko clucking to him, 'O! Katana-san,' ('san' being a Japanese word for a respected man). 'They have been taken away, by a slinking brown creature with a long bushy tail and I do not think they wanted to go because they made much noise.'

Thus Kantana knew that the animal was a fox, and he resolved that he would catch the thief that very night. He set a clever trap and, sure enough, in the morning, there was Master Fox, looking at him through the bars of the cage that he had used as his trap.

'What are you going to do with me, Farmer Kantana-san?' asked the fox, trembling.

'You have shown no mercy to my helpless, innocent chickens,' growled the farmer, 'So, as a punishment, I shall tie ten fireworks to your bushy tail and set fire to them.'

'But, Farmer-san, that is terrible cruelty to a wild animal!' cried the fox. 'I only took the chickens to feed my cubs. What shall they do if you set me on fire?'

'You should have thought of that,' snapped the farmer and he tied ten fat firecrackers to the tail of the fox. Then he set them alight before releasing him from the trap. The fox ran away like a crazy thing, with the fireworks cracking and spluttering on its tail and, because it was so terrified, it ran into the farmer's corn field and set fire to all his corn. So not only did Farmer Kantana Noguchi lose two of his finest chickens but his good harvest went up in smoke and flames. He had taken his revenge on the fox, but his cruelty had cost him dear.

What is more, the fox escaped, perhaps a little bit singed, and ran home to his den.

A pause for thought

There are times when getting your own back may turn out to be a bad thing. Do you always feel better when you have got your own back when someone has annoyed you?

A Haiku for Japanese New Year

Bright chrysanthemums
Flower of the Rising Sun
Smiles at the New Year.

Songs to sing

Changing seasons	*Every Colour* 6
Oshogatsu (till the New Year's here)	*Musical Calendar of Festivals* 10
Father Time	*Sing a Silver Lininge* 25
Think, think on these things	*Sing it in the Morning* 1

85 At the time of a Chinese festival: New Year

Between 21 January and 19 February

Background

The Chinese New Year celebrations begin a week before the New Year begins, with a ceremony in honour of the god of the kitchen. Houses are cleaned, new clothes are worn and everybody resolves to make a fresh start.

The New Year festivities last two weeks and no meat is eaten because the years are named after animals. Special food is eaten, such as dumplings containing gifts (rather as Westerners put coins into Christmas puddings).

Mottoes wishing everyone 'Good Luck' are written on lucky red paper and fixed to doors.

A lot of firecrackers are let off during the two weeks and lanterns are hung in the streets. One of the biggest occasions is the dance of a huge paper lion through the streets, with young men, inside the lion, providing the legs for the dance.

Let's talk

Where is China?

Is China a big or a small country?

Do Chinese people all speak the same language?

Do you have anything in your house made in China?

* *If there are no Chinese children in the school:*

Who knows any Chinese people? Tell us about them.

Tell us anything else you know about China.

(Remember that, at the time of writing, there are two Chinas – the People's Republic and Taiwan)

Tell us anything you know about Hong Kong.

If you have Chinese children in the school, they can, of course, be of great help in the assembly.

Time to listen

Three Giants and a Dragon: a Chinese Story

Long ago, near a little Chinese town called Yanglon, there lived a most terrible dragon. The townspeople were terrified of it. One day, three giants, who were brothers, moved into a castle overlooking the dragon's den.

The youngest brother, Kai, was a small giant, as tall as a bamboo tree and as strong as a horse. The second brother, Chai, was a middle-sized giant, as tall as the top of a walnut tree and as strong as three horses. The third brother, Hai, was a huge giant, as tall as the tallest temple in China and as strong as ten horses.

One day, the giants had to cross the rickety wooden bridge over the river outside the dragon's den. The planks of the bridge creaked, *trip, trap*, as the smallest giant walked across. Out rushed the fearful dragon, blowing flames from its nostrils.

'Who goes there? I am going to gobble you up!' roared the dragon.

Kai called out, 'Oh, don't bother with me, dragon. I am too small. Wait until I have grown more and become big and fat.' The dragon stopped roaring and said that he would wait because he thought that big, fat giants tasted better than thin, small ones. So Kai went on his way.

Then the planks of the rickety wooden bridge creaked, *trip, trap*, as the middle-sized giant walked across. Out rushed the fearful dragon, blowing flames from its nostrils.

'Who goes there? I am going to gobble you up!' roared the dragon. Chai called out, 'Oh, don't bother with me, dragon. I am too small. Wait until I have grown more and become big and fat.' The dragon stopped roaring and said that he would wait because he thought that big, fat giants tasted better than thin, middle-sized ones. So Kai went on his way.

Than along came, Hai, the biggest giant. The dragon was waiting for him, blowing flames from its nostrils.

'Who goes there? I am going to gobble you up!' roared the dragon.

Hai called out, 'That's what you think, stupid dragon.' The dragon stopped roaring because it did not know what to do. While it stood, scratching its scaly head with its sharp claws, Hai walked across the rickety wooden bridge, its planks creaking, *trip, trap*. When he reached the dragon he produced an enormous club and hit the dragon on its scaly head – *bonk*! The dragon fell over, quite dead, Hai went on his way and all the good people of Yanglon were very pleased.

A pause for thought

Bullies often come up against someone bigger or stronger than they are – or someone who is cleverer than they are.

A Tanka for Chinese New Year

Sweep house spotless clean,
Wear the fine new clothes with pride,
Offer Tsao Chun
Sweets, wine, honey for good luck!
Enjoy the lion, dancing.

And

A Haiku for the New Year Lion

Look! Laughing lion!
Lots of legs leaping lightly,
See! Limp, lolling tongue!

Songs to sing

My ship sailed from China	*Apusskidu* 7
Look around	*Every Colour* 9
Chinatown dragon	*Harlequin* 24
New Year greeting	*Musical Calendar of Festivals* 15
New things to do	*Tinderbox* 58
Sing a song of people	*Tinderbox* 18

86 At the time of a Buddhist Festival: the birth of Gautama, the Buddha

April

Background

Buddhists believe it is right for people to live pure and simple lives. This means, therefore, that Buddhists do not ingest substances that can be termed self-abusive, such as alcohol, controlled drugs or tobacco.

This assembly does not seek to offer judgement on the use or abuse of anything in the category, but seeks to introduce children to the concept that one should be careful what goes into one's mouth.

Let's talk

People who are Buddhists do not believe that we should ever kill or hurt living creatures, big or small.

Tell us what you think about this.

Time to listen

The Foolish Yetis

This story has no origins in Buddhist culture or folklore and is only intended to illustrate one of the principles of Buddhist philosophy – that of not using those substances that they regard as noxious – alcohol, tobacco, illegal drugs. How far these sensitive subjects are explored in the classroom is a matter for the policies of individual schools.

Some people believe that strange creatures called Yetis once lived on the slopes of the tallest and snowiest mountains in the world, far away in the country called Tibet; and some people think that they still do. According to the stories, Yetis were (or are) about five times as tall as most of you and covered all over in long, white fur, with just two eyes glittering through the fur.

Perhaps the Yetis had names – nobody knows – but, just for this story, we shall invent some. One day, Yanoo Yeti rushed into Chief Yookoo Yeti's snow hut, calling out in Yeti-speak, 'I've found a new bush growing on the snow slope and its leaves taste wonderful!'

The Chief said, 'Is that so? What does this marvellous fruit look like?'

Yanoo jumped up and down, squeaking excitedly, 'It is a small bush covered with delicious purple leaves!' Chief Yookoo's mouth opened wide, showing his huge teeth.

He stood up to grab Yanoo by his longest fur on the end of his nose and hissed, 'You stupid Yeti! That is the hooslif-hooslif bush and Yetis must never, never, eat its leaves. How many leaves have you eaten?

The frightened Yanoo yelped with pain and said, 'Why, none at all.'

'Good,' said Yookoo, 'Because once a Yeti has eaten the leaves of that bush, they cannot stop. And if they do *not* stop eating the leaves they will go completely … bald! And you know what will happen to a Yeti with no fur on these cold and snowy mountains.'

Yanoo nodded as if his white, furry head would fall off and went on his way. But, oh dear. I am afraid that he had lied to the Chief. He *had* eaten three leaves of the hooslif-hooslif bush and now he wanted more and more. In fact, Yanoo Yeti *had* to have more. He had a feeling inside his head that told him he *must* have more. Yes, he *needed* more.

What happened after that? The silly Yeti spent all his time searching for hooslif-hooslif bushes and, of course, all his fur fell out, he went bald and … well, I expect you can guess the rest. Even worse, all his friends had eaten the leaves of the hooslif-hooslif bush.

So you can understand why it is unlikely that anyone will ever see any more Yetis on the snow slopes of the Himalayan mountains.

**A pause for thought*

Teacher: you must know your audience before asking these questions and responding to the answers.

Why do some people drink a lot of beer or other drinks (soft drinks don't count!)?

Why do they smoke cigarettes?

Do people have other habits that may not be good for them?

A Poem for the Festival of the Birth of Gautama

Besides believing that we should not use harmful substances, Buddhists say that we should not harm any living thing and most certainly not be cruel to them.

This poem suggests that killing or hurting animals for fun is a dreadful thing to do.

Enjoyment

It isn't such fun to squash a fly,
Or poke a kitten in the eye,
Or tie a can to a poor dog's tail,
Or crush a harmless wandering snail;
Their lives aren't yours to take away,
There truly is a better way.

Songs to sing

The animals went in two by two	*Apusskidu* 38
Use your eyes	*Every Colour* 11
Caterpillars only crawl	*Harlequin* 26
The animal fair	*Okki-tokki-unga* 11
I love God's tiny creatures	*Someone's Singing, Lord* 42
Mysteries	*Tinderbox* 40

87 At the time of a Hindu Festival: Raksha Banhan *July/August*

Background

This festival takes place in India at the end of the very rainy part of the year, called the monsoon, on the full moon day of Shravana. There is, of course, no monsoon in this country but the story can be used at any time, especially as the festival will almost certainly fall during school holidays.

The festival is one in which sisters honour their brothers and may be a sensitive subject in certain circumstances – so do your audience research.

Let's talk

If there are no Hindu children in the school:

Who knows any Indian people who are Hindus? Tell us about them.

If you have Hindu children in the school, they can, of course, be involved in the assembly.

Time to listen

Sometimes brothers or sisters can be a nuisance …

Who Needs Sisters?

Perry had three sisters, all born on the same day. Which means they were … ? (*await children's responses*)

That's right – triplets. Camilla, Colette and Cordelia were twice as old as Perry who was aged nine, and he did not like them very much.

Some people might think that he was lucky to have triplets for sisters, but Perry didn't. According to him, all they did was interfere, tease and help themselves to his things. Without asking.

If any one of them wanted a pen or a 10p piece or something, where did they look first and help themselves? In Perry's room. If Camilla's CD player was broken, whose did she borrow? Perry's! If the computer they shared was being used by Colette, whose computer did she borrow? Perry's.

Then, one Saturday morning, he went into his room to watch a TV programme. His TV was missing. A short search showed Cordelia was watching it in the spare bedroom. This was the last straw!

He ran into the kitchen, where his mother was loading the washer. Between sobs he blurted out his troubles which she had heard many times before. He was fed up with being the only boy in the family as well as being the youngest child and, even worse, having three bossy sisters who everybody thought were special because they were triplets, and they teased him and took his things when they felt like it or even if they just felt like annoying him.

His mother smiled and said, calmly, 'Not for much longer.'

Perry gasped, 'What do you mean? Where are they going?'

'They are going away to College next week and you and Dad and Gran and I will have the house to ourselves,' said mother, closing the washer door. Perry could hardly believe the news. Peace at last!

Perry enjoyed it for a whole week. Then he found that his Mum was too busy to play Snakes and Ladders with him, like Camilla used to. There was nobody to read his Harry Potter books to him – Dad was hopeless at it, because he made them sound so boring, not exciting and funny like Colette did. Gran had gone to Bingo, so she could not check his homework like Cordelia always had. It was then that Perry realised that he really missed his sisters. And, when they came home for Christmas holiday, they brought him super presents and didn't tease him too much, so when it was time for them to go back to College in January, he did not want them to go.

As he said, 'I never thought I would miss my sisters. But I do. Even the teasing. And I wouldn't be without them.'

A pause for thought

If you have brothers or sisters, would you miss them if they went away?

A Raksha Bandhan Cinquain about Sisters

Sisters
Can be a pain
To brothers big and small.
While sisters think the same about
Brothers.

Songs to sing

Hari Krishna	*Musical Calendar of Festivals* 93
Consider yourself at home	*Sing a Silver Lining* 16
A time for everything	*Come & Praise* 25
How many people live in your house?	*Tinderbox* 19

88 At the time of a Rastafarian Celebration: Ethiopian New Year

11 September

Background

Rastafari is not a religion but a Christian way of life, and is linked also to Judaism. It takes its name from Ras Tafari who, in 1930, became Haile Selassie, later Emperor of Ethiopia.

Rastafarians believe that Haile Selassie was Jah, their name for God, showing himself as Black King of Africa, and their prophet is Marcus Garvey, born in Jamaica in 1887. He considered that the black people in Jamaica and America, descended from slaves, should be proud of being of African descent.

The story below is about 'drumming' which is an important part of the African heritage of Rastafarians.

Let's talk

**if there are no Rastafarians in school*

Who knows any Rastafarians?

(If someone does) Is there anything you can tell us about the way they look?

If any children are from Rastafarian families, they can, of course, be actively involved in the assembly.

Time to listen

This story has no origins in Rastafarian culture or folklore and is only intended to illustrate one of the aspects of Rastafarian culture.

The Little Drummer Boy

Ten-year old Akaru, who lived far away in the African village of Objano, was mad about drumming and spent all his time listening to the village drummer, Mbembi.

The drummer sent messages over great distances on the drums that he had made himself, for he was also the village drum-maker. Akaru's mother, Alafi, begged him to learn about hunting and fishing because she had to struggle to find enough food for Akaru and herself to eat since his father had died of snake-bite the year before.

Mbembi had given the boy an old set of drums but Akaru had been told by Ofosa, the Headman of the village, that he had to go down to the river to practise where only the crocodiles could hear his dreadful row.

One day, Alafi called her son to catch a fish for dinner because she had no money to go to market. Grumbling, because he had planned to play his old drums, Akaru went down to the river to practise sending messages on his old drums.

He decided to pretend drumming the message, 'Clear the village, herd of elephants charging towards you'. Nothing like this had ever happened in Objano village, so it was quite safe to pretend to send such a message. No-one would believe it.

The little drummer boy had just started, and hit one drum, when he was astonished to hear the sound of angry elephants trumpeting and screaming. Then he heard a rumbling, thundering noise and the earth began to shake.

It really was a herd of elephants, charging towards the village. Akaru whipped off the blankets and began thumping out his practice message for real: 'Clear the village! Herd of elephants charging towards you!' Of course, sad to say, but only to be expected, nobody in the village believed that the message was real, not even Drummer Mbembi. Until forty charging elephants arrived and everyone had to run for their lives.

Every hut in the village was flattened although nobody was hurt. Akaru was very upset because he was grumbled at for not warning anybody about the elephants, which seemed a bit unfair.

As he said, 'There's no pleasing some people.'

A pause for thought

As well as enjoying drumming, Rastafarians are vegetarians, which means they eat no meat. Think of some reasons why people become vegetarians.

A poem about Rastfarians' hair-styles

Rastafarians, like Sikhs, do not cut their hair. Instead, they have it fashioned into fine plaits that take a hairdresser a long time to do.

Dreadlocks

Twisting, plaiting, weaving,
sitting patiently
In the chair
As Mistress Honey
shows her flair
And braids my hair
into a miracle
of sculpture.
And joy! joy! joy!
She will not need
to torture me again
for ages!

Songs to sing

Sing and jump for joy	*Mango Spice* 34
Banyan tree	*Music Box Song Book* 20
Hair	*Music Box Song Book* 30
Put your finger on your head	*Okki-tokki-unga* 27
Jamaica farewell	*Ta-ra-ra-boom-de-ay* 17
Kaigal – hands	*Tinderbox* 4

89 At the time of a Sikh Festival: the birthday of Guru Gobind Singh

December/January

Background

In 1699, Guru Gobind Singh began the Khalsa, the name given to Sikhs who are full members of the Sikh religion and means 'the pure ones'. Guru Gobind Singh was born in 1675 and his birthday is celebrated by Sikhs all over the world.

Processions through the streets often take place and five people usually lead the procession. This is to remember the five men who were the first to join the Khalsa.

Let's talk

**If there are no Sikhs in school.*

Who knows any Sikhs?

(If someone does) Is there anything you can tell us about the way the men and boys look after their hair?

If any children are from Sikh families, they can, of course, be actively involved in the assembly

Time to listen

This story has no origins in Sikh culture or folklore and is only intended to illustrate one of the principles of Sikh philosophy – that no person is better than another.

Six Little Tadpoles

Six tadpoles lived happily in a pond of clear water. That is, until Tiddly Tadpole started to grow a pair of back legs, as all tadpoles do as they begin to change into … frogs.

Tiddly told his brothers and sisters that, because he now had legs and they did not, that made him more important than they were and so he was to be called 'Boss Tadpole.'

'I'm not calling you Boss Tadpole,' sneered Tussy Tadpole, 'You're no different from any of us.'

Tiddly gave her a sneaky little kick with one of his new legs and said boastfully, 'Look, there's more of me than there is of you now. So 'Boss' it is. Or else I shall kick you with the other leg.' The other tadpoles did not like it but they agreed to use the new name – until next day when Tinker Tadpole woke up and found he had got a pair of tiny back legs, too!

Now, you couldn't have *two* tadpoles called 'Boss Tadpole', could you? Then, one by one, each tadpole grew a new pair of back legs and there was no more talk of 'Boss' tadpoles. Until Tiddly found his *front* legs were growing and he started all over again, only this time he wanted to be called 'Lord Tadpole'. Nobody did and anyway, next day, the other five tadpoles all found *they* had back and front legs, too.

Then Tiddly found that his tail was shrinking and he realised that he was now the first tailless tadpole in the pond which, in his opinion, made him more important than the others. And they were to call him, 'King Tadpole'. But before the other tadpoles could argue about it, Daisy Duck put her head under water.

'Hello', she said, 'Did I hear you say 'King' Tadpole?'

Tiddly said, 'Yes. I am more important than the others now. First back legs, first front legs. And now, first to lose tail. Yes, I'm King, all right.'

'Jolly good,' said Duck, cheerily, 'I'll eat you first, then.' Which she did. By the time she had swallowed King Tadpole, the others had swum into the mud at the bottom of the pond. There they told each other than no tadpole was better than another tadpole. Especially when they would all turn into frogs one day. Unless Daisy Duck got them first.

A pause for thought

Is one person really any better than another? Is that the same as being more important than another person?

What makes one person more important than another?

An Unfriendly Tanka!

Who's better than who

Oi. You with the face,
Who you looking at then? Me?
Think you are better
Than I am? Perhaps you are,
Pal. Just don't say it out loud.

Songs to sing

A better world	*Alleluya* 60
On life's highway	*Every Colour* 28
Can you hear?	*Harlequin* 33
Just the same	*Songs for Every Day* 16
Sun arise	*Tinderbox* 43

90 At the time of Rosh Hashanah, the Jewish New Year *September/October*

Background

The Book of Exodus in the Old Testament describes how Moses brought the Jewish people to Mount Sinai after their escape from slavery in Egypt. There, God told Moses what laws they should follow – beginning with the ten most important, the Ten Commandments.

Let's talk

**If there are no Jewish children in school:*

Who knows any Jewish people?

(If someone does) Tell us what you know about them.

If any children are from Jewish families, they can, of course, be actively involved in the assembly.

Time to listen

This story takes the Ninth Commandment as its foundation.

In biblical language: Thou shalt not bear false witness against thy neighbour.

In everyday language: You should not make up untrue stories about people you know.

This story has no origins in Jewish culture or folklore and is only intended to illustrate one of the principles of Jewish philosophy.

Oo, I Never!

Momma Grouchy Bear stormed into the living room of the den, startling the three little cubs who were watching Bear TV.

'Who's been at this honey pot?' she demanded to know, holding out a sticky and almost empty honey pot.

Nobody answered at first, then Boofa and Binky both pointed, at the same time, at Beeny.

'She did,' they chorused.

'Momma, I never did,' wailed Beeny, 'They are both telling whopper fibs!'

Momma interrupted, 'I am very disappointed with you, Beeny. No supper until you tell me the truth. Go to your room and have a big bear-think,' and off she went.

'Hee hee hee,' sniggered Boofa and Binky, 'That paid you back for not doing our homework for us when we asked you.'

Beeny rushed out of the room, wailing, 'Oo, you're always telling lies about me to save your own furry skins!'

A few days later, when the three little bears were playing Bears-and-Ladders, they heard Momma roaring from the kitchen, 'Come in here at once, you naughty little bear cubs!' They crept in to see Momma looking very angry.

'Right,' she growled, her nose twitching with fury, 'Who's been at the eggs?' (Perhaps you don't know it, but Grouchy Bears love *raw* eggs. Yes, I think 'Yik', too. But then I'm not a Grouchy Bear.)

Binky and Boofa pointed their little claws at Beeny and said, together,

'It was her, Momma, it was her! We saw her, Momma. we saw her.'

Momma looked very angry as she rumbled, 'Is that so now? Well, why have you two got egg yolk all over your greedy little snouts? I think you are two wicked little bear cubs, telling lies about your sister. It was you who ate the eggs. And you know more about the honey pot than she does.'

I won't tell you what Momma did next, but two little bears had two sore little sit-down-upons for a few days after that, so I expect you can guess what happened. Ouch!

A pause for thought

What can happen if you tell lies about someone you know?

A Poem about telling lies

Little Lies

One day I told a little lie
That grew and grew and grew;
It filled my bedroom and the loft,
The bathroom and the loo.
It squashed itself into the lounge
The kitchen and the hall;
And then slid out under the door
And climbed the garden wall.
It covered gardens, houses, roads,
And then engulfed the city;
It sludged itself on hills and dales
And stopped them looking pretty.
And now I know that little lies
Grow big, just like Mum said;
Don't think I'll tell another one,
I'll try the truth instead.

Carol Rumble

Songs to sing

A better world	*Alleluya* 60
Zum, gali, gali	*Music Box Song Book* 78
It's a new day	*Come & Praise* 106
I jump out of bed in the morning	*Okki-Tokki-unga* 47
Water come a me eye	*Mango Spice* 28
One, two, three	*Tinderbox* 65

91 At the time of a Muslim Festival: Eid-al-Adha

No Western calendar equivalent

Background

Islam teaches, among other good qualities, that generosity to people less well off than you are is something that all good Muslims should try to do. This is the duty called *Zakat*, the fifth pillar of Islam.

Eid-al-Alha is the major festival of the Islamic Year and is 'the feast of the sacrifice'.

Special prayers are held in the morning and children may accompany parents. In the UK, many Muslims give money for feeding the poor, instead of buying an animal to sacrifice, although some make special arrangements for sacrificing an animal in an abbatoir, according to Islamic law.

Let's talk

None suggested.

Time to listen

There are times when you will feel better if you are not mean when you can afford to be generous.

Do Unto Others

Uncle Ebenezer had died and left all his money to his nephew Tarquin Trumple, although they had never met. The young man decided to leave his tiny flat, where he lived alone with his cat, Willow, of whom he was very fond.

Tarquin bought a huge house with twenty bedrooms and a swimming pool, and moved in. He was annoyed that Willow did not seem to like the big house and she ran away, back to the tiny flat, where she knew all the smells and had her own catty friends. Mrs Bliss, the old lady who had moved into the flat, loved cats and she adopted Willow.

Tarquin tried to tempt Willow back to live with him, but it was no good. The cat liked her old home and her new mistress and that was that. Then, one day, he had a phone call from Mrs Bliss.

'Oh, Mr Trumple, sir, your dear, poor pussy-cat is ill and I need some money to take her to a vet. Can you help me. please? I am too poor to pay vet's bills and I only need £20.'

Tarquin snorted in disgust, 'You've got a cheek,' he said, angrily. 'The stupid cat won't come and live with me. Why should I do anything for the silly animal when it prefers to stay with you? Pay for it yourself,' and he slammed the phone down.

Sadly, Willow died and Mrs Bliss rang Tarquin to tell him. It was a shock to Tarquin and he told the old woman that he was terribly sorry because he really had loved Willow.

'I am so upset, Mrs Bliss,' he whimpered. 'Let me give you some money to buy a bigger flat, because yours is very small. And another cat. Two, if you like and I shall give £1000 to any cats' home you like.'

Mrs Bliss said, sadly, 'That's very kind of you, sir, but it won't bring Willow back, will it?' It was then that Tarquin realised how foolish he had been. But no matter how he tried, he could not forgive himself,

A pause for thought

Being sorry is not much help when you have done something very selfish and it cannot be put right, however hard you try.

A Haiku about being mean

Surely comes the day,
When all the sad, mean people
Hide shameful faces.

Songs to sing

Both sides now	*Alleluya* 33
We are climbing	*Come & Praise* 49
Because you care	*Every Colour* 31
Look up	*New Child Songs* 1
Who will buy?	*Sing a Silver Lining* 12
Mysteries	*Tinderbox* 40

PART IV
APPENDICES

APPENDIX 1

Prayers for use by children or teachers

Schools, rightly or wrongly, interpret 'an act of corporate worship' in different ways – not all schools use prayers during every assembly. For that reason, prayers have been not been included in the main text of each assembly. Instead, Appendix 1 comprises a selection of prayers related to section headings, rather than individual assemblies.

The method of using the prayers is left to the conducting teacher – the text is simple enough for children to repeat aloud after the teacher, if desired.

The 'School Creeds' are intended to be communally spoken and therefore should be committed to memory. Two versions are set to music on pages 227–8.

The two versions of the Lord's Prayer on page 225 are also intended for communal speaking.

The family of school

Hello, God. Thank you for a safe journey to school. Help us to do our best today.

We thank you, Father, for our school and for the new friends that we shall make here.

God, our Father, teach us to be polite to our teachers and their helpers and to other grown-ups in school.

Hello, God, help us to know that our teachers are our friends.

Father God, help us not to be afraid to ask our teachers and their helpers if we need help.

Dear God, we know that all the people who work in this school are only here so that we may learn about the world around us.

Thank you, God, for our teachers and everybody who works in this school.

Father of us all, show us how to treat everybody with kindness and good manners.

Hello, God, We thank you today for our school family. We are happy to belong here and will do our best for the family.

Are you listening, God? Show us that, although children may come from homes that are different from our own, that we are all your children and that you love each and every one of us.

Father God, help us to understand that some other children may be different from us in some ways. Help us to be their friends.

Dear Lord, help to make the people of the world one family and help us to love our brothers and sisters all over the world.

Dear Father God, thank you for all the toys and other things we use in school to learn about your world.

Are you listening, God? Please look after us today and every day and keep us safe.

Dear Lord, take care of us when we work and play. Teach us to do as our teachers ask without grumbling.

Dear God,
Help us to do the things we should,
To be to others kind and good;
In all we do at school or play,
To grow more loving every day.

Father of us all, please bless our school and help us to do all we can to make it even better than it is now.

Just you

Thank you, Father God, for birthdays and for the chanc to become wiser as we grow older.

God, our Father, teach us to act in a way that shows how old we are. Help us not to depend too much on grown-ups and older children.

Hello, God. We hope you are happy in your home. Make us grateful for our homes and the love that we know is there.

Thank you, God, for our families and the homes where we live. Teach us to do all we can to help at home.

Father God, teach us to eat and sleep properly so that we become healthy grown-ups.

Dear God, make us brave to visit dentists and doctors. We know know that they are skilful people who will do their best for us and give us the benefit of their knowledge.

Are you listening, God? Remind us to do those things which we must do to keep ourselves clean and healthy.

Father, teach us to play only in places which we know are safe and where we will come to no harm. Help us never to put other people in danger because of our own foolish behaviour.

God our Father, make us sensible children who will never worry our parents or guardians by doing foolish things or dangerous things.

Dear God, who cares for us all, make sure we never leave the places where we play, with strangers, however tempting it may be.

Lord, teach us to take care of the toys and other things we are given. Let us never be ungrateful for being given the things that give us pleasure.

Family and you

Father God, Thank you for our families. Show us how to play our part by being good and helpful children.

Show us, Father, show us how to do things for ourselves when we are able. Teach us not to rely on others to do them for us if there is no need.

Hello, God. Make us sensible children who realise that we are not the only ones who matter in our family.

Dear Lord, teach us that we can be much happier at home and at school if we do not squabble or quarrel about unimportant things.

Lord God, thank you for my friends. Help me to keep promises I make to them and not to let them down.

Are you listening, God? Show us how to understand that, in a competition, someone must win and others must lose. Teach us not to sulk if we do not win every time.

Father, be proud of us when we work hard to make our school and homes tidy and free of litter.

Older people (eg grandparents)

Lord, teach us to show respect to older people like our grandparents, because we can learn a great deal from them.

Father God, please look after our grandparents and keep them safe and happy.

Dear God, let us never be impatient with older people. Help us to remember that many of them cannot get about as quickly as we can.

Pets

Please, God, thank you for our pets. Help us to take care of cats and dogs and other animals. Teach us never to be cruel to them.

God, our Father, let us never be cruel to our pets by not feeding them properly or by not keeping them clean.

Please, God, let us never forget that animals cannot talk to us to tell us when something is wrong.

Growing up

Hello, God. Teach us to be polite to others, even if we do not know them.

Lord, teach us to be patient, however hard it may be to have to wait.

Father, help us to think before we do something, whether it is at work or at play.

Are you nice to know?

Are you listening, God? Only you know that we are often tempted to tell a lie. Make us strong to tell the truth at all times.

Dear Father God, we are your children. Please make us wise so that we do nothing dishonest, especially if it might hurt other people.

Dear God, help us not to think we are better than we are but to remember that you are great and we are very small.

Father, when it comes to tackling a new task, help us to realise that we may need help at some time.

Dear God, help us to do our best at all times, inside and outside the classroom.

God, our Father, when we want to give up, help us to try a little harder. Help us, too, to know when it is time to say we cannot solve a problem and to ask for help.

Lord, let us never be unkind to others.

Please, God, teach us never to tease or to bully other children, whether we are in or out of school.

Father God, please help us to see that teasing and bullying is wrong and cruel and that it makes children very unhappy.

Please forgive us, God, if we have ever teased or bullied other children. We promise that we will never do it again.

The place where we live

Father of us all, help us to respect the places where we live. Let us never damage or destroy property that belongs to others or to all of us.

Dear God, teach us never to damage or break things just for fun.

Lord, teach us to respect other people's houses and gardens.

Thank you, Father God, for parks and playing fields and all green places where we and others enjoy ourselves.

God bless our villages and towns and cities. Help us to keep them clean and free of damage.

Family of nature

Hello, God. Today we thank you for the world of Nature.
For sun and rain,
For woods and fields,
For sea and sky.

For flowers and birds and butterflies
And for all your gifts to us,
Everything around is full of joy,
Help us to be joyful, too and give us thankful hearts.

Thank you, Lord, for your wonderful world, for flowers and trees and for the animals that share our world.

Thank you for the world so sweet,
Thank you for the food we eat;
Thank you for the birds that sing,
Thank you, God, for everything.

People who look after us

We thank you, dear Father, for fireman and ambulance crews who are always on duty, ready to help us.

We are grateful, Lord, for those men and women who risk their lives when there is fire or accident.

We thank you, Father God, for all those men and women who care for us when we are ill – for doctors and nurses who work in hospitals and in the ambulance service we give you thanks.

Thank you, Lord, for our family doctors who work in our towns and villages. Bless them and their work in caring for sick people in their surgeries and in their patients' homes.

Dear God, thank you for doctors and nurses who tend people who need special care when they are very ill.

Father of us all, we thank you for all people who do unpleasant jobs to make our lives more comfortable. We are grateful for people who take away our rubbish and for those who work in sewage works.

Lord, teach us to be grateful for those people who do dangerous or unpleasant jobs of all kinds.

Hello, God. Today we thank you for our teachers. Thank you for the hard work that they do in teaching us. Help us to be sensible children so that our school can be a happy place where we can learn all the things we need to know.

Prayers for special days

New Year

Hello, God, we are at the beginning of a New Year. Help us to be good and sensible children through the year that has now begun.

Lord, take care of all those whom we love during this New Year and all the years yet to come.

Shrove Tuesday

Father God, teach us to remember that Pancake Day is not just a time for eating pancakes but a time when we tell you that we are sorry for the things we have done.

Mother's Day

*We thank you, God, for our mothers and for all the care and love that they give to us. Help us to show them that we love them by being caring and loving children.

Easter

Lord, help us to remember that Easter is a special time to all Christians, when they remember what happened to Jesus Christ. It is not just an excuse for eating chocolate eggs.

May Day

Lord, may we enjoy the holiday that is May Day. Thank you for the celebrations that remind us that spring is on the way.

**Father's Day*

We thank you, God, for our fathers and for all they do for us. Help us to repay them, by being loving and sensible children.

Harvest Festival

All good gifts around us
Are sent from heaven above,
Then thank the Lord, O thank the Lord,
For all his love.

Father God, we thank you for our daily bread and for the farmers that grow the wheat to make it. Thank you, too, for all the fruit and vegetables that are harvested in our country and abroad.

Lord, take care of the brave men who risk their lives at sea to bring us fish from dangerous seas.

Hallowe'en

Make us wise, Father, so that we do not worry people when we enjoy our 'Trick and Treat' fun. Give us the sense to realise that old and nervous people may not share our jokes.

Bonfire Night

Lord, help us to help ourselves to stay safe on Bonfire Night.

Father, teach us that we should never take risks with fireworks and bonfires.

Dear God, remind us to take care of our pets on Bonfire Night so they will not be frightened.

Christmas time

We thank you, Father, for everything we enjoy at Christmas time.

Look after us, God, as we begin our Christmas holiday. Teach us to think of others during this happy time and to do our best to help grown-ups at home.

At this joyful time, Father, help us to think of those children and grown-ups who will not be able to enjoy this Christmas because they are too ill or too poor.

Father God, look after those people who have to work at Christmas time so that we may have light and warmth in our homes.

Thank you God, for the birthday of Jesus, which we celebrate at Christmas time.

Saints' Days

Father of all people, we thank you for the saints of our countries. Thank you especially for Saint (David, Patrick, George, Andrew) and for the work they did long ago to teach us about you and your great love.

Father of all people, we thank you for all the saints. Help us to find out all we can about the countries to which their names have become important and about the people who live there.

General prayers for all occasions

Hello, God. Please teach us to be grateful for each day that dawns.

Father God, help us to make the best of each day that you give us.

Are you listening, God? Teach us that we cannot do what we like when we like.

Lord, help me to be brave when I am afraid.

Dear Father, help us to do all the good we can in all the ways we can.

Thank you, Father, for health and strength.

Hello, God. Please teach us what is right and what is wrong.

Father God, be good to me. I am so small and the world is so big.

Our Father, as we begin another day, Help us in all we do and say.

A School Creed 1 (following the theme of 'Family')

This is our school
And we are family;
Let us promise together
That this shall be a happy place,
Where we love one another
As brothers and sisters;
Let us promise together
That this shall be a happy place,
Where we can learn
About the world around us.

A School Creed 2 (following the theme of 'Building')

This is our school,
Let peace live here,
Let the rooms be full of happiness.
Let love be all around,
Love of one another,
Love of all people,
And love of life and living.
Let us remember
That, as many hands build a house,
So many hearts build a school.

Both Creeds are set to music on pages 227 and 228 in this Appendix

A Child's Prayer 1 (based on the Lord's Prayer)

God, our Father who loves the world,
We say your name with wonder;
You are with us now and for ever.
May we do what You want us to do
And be what You want us to be,
Please feed us and do not let us be thirsty;
We are sorry if we have done wrong
And we will feel sorry for people
Who have hurt us,
Help us to be good children
And keep us safe, always.

A Child's Prayer 2 (based on the Lord's Prayer)

Father God, who is everywhere,
Your name is very special;
You are with us now
And always will be.
Please care for us because we are small
And you are great.
We are sorry for doing wrong things
And we will try to forgive others
Just as you forgive us.
Make us good children
And keep us safe from harm.

The Lord's Prayer (Matthew 6, New English version, 1970)

Our Father in heaven,
thy name be hallowed;
they kingdom come,
thy will be done,
on earth as in heaven.
Give us today our daily bread.
Forgive us the wrong we have done,
as we have forgiven those who have wronged us.
And do not bring us to the test,
But save us from the evil one.
Amen.

Prayers for the Close of School

O let us see another day
Bless us all this night we pray,
And to the sun we all will bow
And say, 'Goodbye' but just for now.

(part of the Reverend. Eli Jenkins' sunset prayers to Llareggub Hill, from Under Milk Wood *by Dylan Thomas)*

Now the day is over,
The dark will soon be here
Lord, keep us safe all through the night
Till morning light appears.

Goodnight to school,
School day is nearly past,
God keep us safe as we go home
Our lessons done at last.

Blessings for the close of school

Father God, keep us safe as we make our way home.

Lord, take care of through this night.

Dear God, we thank you for today and look forward to tomorrow.

May God bless us and keep us through this night and in all the days yet to come.

May God bless us and keep us safe in all that we do now and always.

APPENDIX 2

Music to the School Creeds

We Are Family

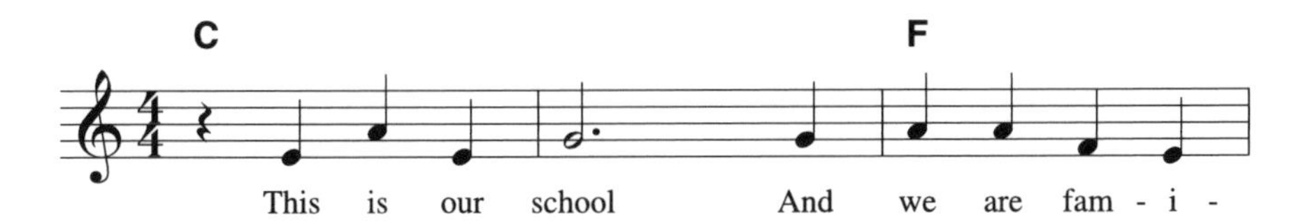

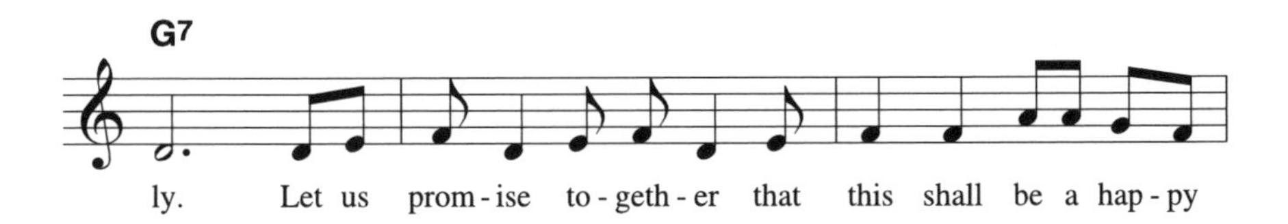

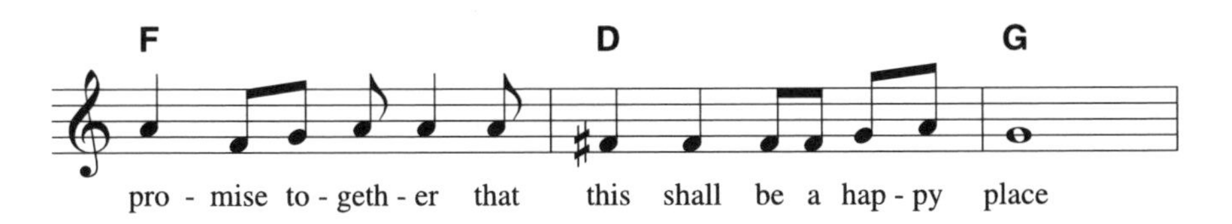

A School Creed

APPENDIX 3

Source song books

Published by	*Title*
A & C Black	*Alleluya* *Apusskidu* *Carol, gaily Carol* *Flying a Round* *Harlequin* *The Jolly Herring* *Mango Spice* *Okki-tokki-unga* *Play School Song Book* *Sing a Silver Lining* *Someone's Singing, Lord* *Ta-ra-ra-boom-de-ay* *Tinderbox*
BBC	*Come & Praise* *Music Box Song Book*
Collins	*Multi-coloured Music Bus*
Holt, Rinehart & Wilson	*Sing a Song of Celebration*
Nelson	*Sing it in the Morning*
Out of the Ark Music	*Songs for Every Day* *Songs for Every Season*
Ward Lock Educational	*Alphabet Zoo Book* *Silly Aunt Sally* *Every Colour under the Sun*

Suggestions for additional songs

Family of School

The building song	*Come & Praise*	61
Look around	*Every Colour*	9
On life's highway	*Every Colour*	28
Magic Penny	*Sing it in the Morning*	7
Happy talk	*Sing a Silver Lining*	3
Morning has broken	*Someone's Singing, Lord*	3
Monday morning	*Songs for Every Day*	6

Just You

On a work day I work	*Every Colour*	24
Because you can	*Every Colour*	31
Guess how I feel	*Come & Praise*	89
I may speak	*Come & Praise*	100
Johnny get your hair combed	*Music Box Song Book*	13
So do I(hate washing)	*Music Box Song Book*	25
You and I	*Tinderbox*	56

Family and You

The supper-supper march	*Apusskidu*	6
Travel on	*Come & Praise*	42
Every colour under the sun	*Every Colour*	16
Hodge's Grace	*Flying a Round*	37
Consider yourself at home	*Sing a Silver Lining*	16
You are my sunshine	*Ta-ra-ra-boom-de-ay*	16
I've got a body	*Tinderbox*	5
Apusski dusky	*Apusskidu*	51
Lollipop Man	*Flying a Round*	7

Growing Up

One more step	*Come & Praise*	72
Would you turn your back?	*Every Colour*	34
We will take care of you	*Every Colour*	36
Who will buy?	*Sing a Silver Lining*	12
Newspaper pictures	*Songs for Every Day*	46
I would like to be	*Tinderbox*	45
Try again	*Tinderbox*	56

Are You Nice to Know?

Do your best	*Every Colour*	48
Think of a world	*Come & Praise*	17
It's a new day	*Come & Praise*	106
We want to sing	*Sing a Silver Lining*	7
Taking my time	*Songs for Every Day*	61
All alone in my quiet head	*Tinderbox*	17
Love somebody	*Tinderbox*	16

The Place Where We Live

Song	Book	Page
Look around	*Every Colour*	9
Coal-hole cavalry	*Jolly Herring*	9
What's it like in the place where you live?	*Play School Song Book*	14
We want to sing	*Sing a Silver Lining*	13
Hosanna	*Mango Spice*	25
Linstead Market	*Ta-ra-ra-boom-de-ay*	19
Skyscraper Wean	*Tinderbox*	36

Family of Nature

Song	Book	Page
All things bright and beautiful	*Come & Praise*	3
Country life	*Flying a Round*	60
Snowdrop bells	*Harlequin*	11
It happens each Spring	*Harlequin*	15
Leave them a flower	*Jolly Herring*	17
God bless the grass	*Someone's Singing, Lord*	27
The flowers that grow in the garden	*Someone's Singing, Lord*	53

People who Look After Us

Song	Book	Page
The guard song	*Apusskidu*	32
The family of man	*Come & Praise*	69
Because you care	*Every Colour*	31
There's room enough for you	*Every Colour*	33
Lollipop man	*Flying a Round*	7
Penny Lane	*Jolly Herring*	67
Litterbin song	*Play School Song Book*	27

APPENDIX 4
Suggestions for background music

('Mood' music for arrival at and departing from the Assembly area)

Schools usually have their own ideas about atmospheric or 'mood' music – for children aged between 4 and 8, music chosen is most likely to be regarded by them as 'Musak', unless teachers actively encourage children to listen to what is being played. Many schools 'post' the choice of music for the day or week in a prominent place.

The choice of music that eventually arrives on a school's audio equipment is likely to be influenced by the range of the school's resources. For that reason the following suggestions can do no more than indicate the type of music which will help to put children in a receptive frame of mind for what they are about to receive from headteacher or teacher and also add to a calm atmosphere as they head for clasrooms and the day's business.

Instrumental music or simple vocals that appeal to children are the most obvious choice, unless the teacher has a particular path to pursue.

Theme tunes and songs from TV programmes are popular, even though the programmes may now only appear on home videos – Postman Pat, Fireman Sam, Ivor the Engine, Teletubbies, *et al*, still have an appreciative juvenile audience.

Standard pop songs are to be found it on compilation or remixes, either as tapes or discs. Remixes by modern artists often appeal to children of all ages.

Examples of 'Background' Music

Classical

Coates	Three Bears Suite
Chopin	Fantasie Impromptu
Debussy	Children's Corner Suite
Delius	Summer Evening
Diniculu	Hora Stacata
Dvorak	Humoresque
Elgar	Cockaigne Overture
Faure	Dolly Suite
Hadyn	Clock Symphony(2nd movement)
Havegal Brian	Trotting to Market
Mozart	Toy Symphony

Ravel	Pavane pour une infante defunte
Orff	O Fortuna
Saint-Saens	The Swan
Schumann	Carnaval
Tchaikowsky	Nutcracker Suite
Vaughan-Williams	The Lark Ascending

Excerpts and Themes from Stage/Film Musicals

Any Andrew Lloyd-Webber musicals
eg *Cats, Chess, Godspell, Joseph and the Amazing Technicolor Dreamcoat, Whistle down the Wind*

Stage

Hair, Moulin Rouge, Oklahoma, West Side Story

Film

Bambi	*The 101 Dalmatians,*	*Fantasia*
The Jungle Book	*The King and I*	*Limelight*
The Lion King	*The Little Mermaid,*	*Mary Poppins*
Peter Pan	*Snow White and the Seven Dwarfs*	
Star Wars	*Watership Down*	*Dr Zhivago*

TV/Radio

Themes from: The Archers, Ballykissangel, Brookside, Eastenders Emmerdale, Heartbeat, The Little House on the Prairie, The Waltons

Pop music

Contemporary pop music, with some exceptions, tends to be emphemeral and, in many cases, instantly forgettable. Some tunes, mostly elderly, seem to re-emerge from time to time as cover versions as new soloists and groups create their own versions of standards. The following examples are typical. Performers, rather than composers, have been listed, but almost every song in the lists has been performed by other artists at some time or another.

Artist	*Song*
Abba	Arrival
Armstrong, Louis	What a wonderful world
Atwell, Winifred	Britannia Rag
Ball, Kenny	March of the Siamese children
Beatles	Here comes the sun
Bilk, Acke	Stranger on the shore
Brett, Adrian	Sailing
Chas and Dave	Rabbit
Conway, Russ	Roulette
Crosby, Bing	Swingin' on a star
Dorsey, Tommy	On the sunny side of the street
Edward, Cliff	When you wish upon a star
Goons,The	The Ying-Tong Song
Harris, Rolf	Tie me kangaroo down, sport
Inman, John	Teddy Bears' Picnic
Whistling Jack Smith	I was Kaiser Bill's batman
New Vaudeville Band	Winchester Cathedral
Nicola LeFanu	Invisible places
Oldfield, Mike	Tubular Bells
Ornandel, Cyril	Tale of Peter Rabbit
Rose, David(Orch)	Holiday for strings
Scaffold	Lily the Pink
Semprini	Kitten on the Keys
The Spinners	Family of Man
Strings for Pleasure	Pink Panther Theme
Status Quo	Whatever you want
Jimmy Shand	Bluebell Polka
Paul Tapp	Tubby the Tuba
Tacticos and his Bousoukis	Zorba the Greek

APPENDIX 5

Useful assembly books for further reference

Source/Author	***Title and Publishers***
NB Some of these books are out of print	
Brandling	*Assemblies for Primary Schools* *Spring, Summer, Autumn, Winter Assembly Books* *Good, Morning, Everybody!* (Stanley Thornes) *This Morning's Story* (Nash Pollock)
Barrett	*Tinderbox Assembly Book* (A & C Black)
Cooling	*Assemblies for Primary Schools, Autumn, Spring & Summer Terms* *Wisdom for Worship* (REMP)
Davies	*Many Hearts* *See, Another Day* (Nash Pollock)
Farncombe	*It's Our Assembly* *It's Our Turn for Assembly* *Let's Plan an Assembly* (National Council for Christian Education)
Fisher	*The Assembly Year* (Collins) *Together Today* (Evans)
Jackson	*Join with Us 1 & 2* *Share Our World* (Stanley Thornes)
Price & Parmiter	*A World of Light* (Schofield & Sims)
Purton	*Day by Day* (Nash Pollock)
Purton & Storey	*First Assemblies* (Simon & Schuster)
Tracey & Dinsdale	*Active Assemblies for the National Curriculum* (Schofield & Sims)
Vause	*Infant Assembly Book*
Ward	*Assemblies A-Z* (Stanley Thornes)
Wilcock	*Through the Year* (Stanley Thornes)
Wood	*Assembly Kit* (Longman)